Office Christianity

Perry E. White

OFFICE CHRISTIANITY

Living out your faith in your workplace

BROADMAN PRESS
NASHVILLE, TENNESSEE

© Copyright 1990 ● Broadman Press

All rights reserved

4260-24

ISBN: 0-8054-6024-1

Dewey Decimal Classification: 248.4

Subject Heading: CHRISTIAN LIFE

Library of Congress Catalog Card Number: 90-31942

Printed in the United States of America

Scripture quotations are from the *Revised Standard Version* of the Bible, copyrighted 1946, 1952, © 1971, 1973.

Library of Congress Cataloging-in-Publication Data

White, Perry E., 1926-

    Office Christianity / Perry E. White.

      p. cm.

    ISBN: 0-8054-6024-1 :

    1. Witness bearing (Christianity) 2. Work--Religious aspects--Christianity. I Title.

    BV4520. W47 1990

90-31942

CIP

To Helen

Contents

Preface

As one of the estimated 50 million who work in offices, I hope that my Christian faith is a leaven to all aspects of my life. However, as fallible human beings we all tend to departmentalize our lives so that our jobs, recreation, homelife, and faith may have little to do with each other.

If we claim to follow Christ and make God our Guide, we accept the responsibility of educating, feeding, and caring for others as well as ourselves, regardless of what we may be doing at the moment. "Be proud of that and get at it," a ministering friend of mine told me.

This collection of inspirational thoughts is an attempt to relate personal experiences, the experiences of others, and ideas picked up from various sources which are applicable to the huge army of people who work in offices. To those who punch keyboards, operate telephone switchboards, run the office copying machines, or rummage through files with insistent regularity, this book is written.

Whether your office job is good, bad, or boring, the aim of these pages is to help in looking at the joys and frustrations of your work in the light of Christian faith.

I truly hope you will be able to find something of what

God may be saying to you through the thoughts God has given me.

Perry E. White
December 31, 1988
Moore, Oklahoma

Introduction

    This book can be read meaningfully in at least three ways.

    It can be read straight through in sequence so the ideas can build on and complement each other. The reader can pick out the chapters which are most meaningful and then go back to the others. Or the book can be used as a reference, picking out chapters which can help at a particular time of need.

    Other than the first two chapters and possibly the final three chapters, the subject matter is presented in no particular order. They were written in the order the author experienced them or was reminded of them by others, and as ideas from reading and conversations which sparked fond and not-so-fond memories.

    No doubt, not every possible situation is covered. And some situations, which seem to be mentioned more than once, are considered from differing angles and depths.

    I sincerely hope these thoughts and inspirations will be of help in your journey through life, as they have been for me.

1
The Office Family

You may scoff at the idea that an office full of people can become a family. There may not be one other fellow employee in that office you would voluntarily choose as a relative. But then, if you think about it, can you name every member of your extended biological and in-law family as a personal friend? Probably not.

The office family is a different kind of family. For one thing, you are not absolutely required to stay as a member of that family. Presumably there are jobs elsewhere with other, maybe more appealing, office families.

The reactions within the office family may not be as intense as with favorite members of your biological family, yet members often experience emotional feelings when a member suffers a hardship, becomes ill, or has some traumatic experience.

Jesus teaches us that God includes all humankind as His family. If each of us accepted that concept, how far could the world go in relieving injustice, hunger, and the consequences from being unloved?

This is the concept which underlies the pages of this book.

PRAYER: It is difficult, God, to look upon everyone in this world as a child of Yours. The "unlovable," those who hurt others, and those who withdraw make it seem impossible they could be potentially your children. Yet, if we

follow Your lead and the example Jesus gave us, we must
try. Oh, we must try. Amen.

2
Loving the Office Family

Loving others as ourselves, a key teaching of Jesus, can
be expressed toward fellow workers in friendliness, even
fondness, making the work and the work area more
enjoyable.

Two men flared at each other over a matter which was
so insignificant that neither can now remember what it
was. Immediately after the argument, hard feelings en-
sued and neither had anything to say to the other for several days.

Finally, one decided the situation needed correcting
and worked mentally to put himself in the other's shoes.
He found himself developing a feeling of empathy with
the other.

In a forgiving attitude, conversation and relationships
gradually redeveloped. It was not long before the two men
were amiable again.

This is an example of effective use of the two command-
ments which Jesus stressed most often—loving God and
loving others.

PRAYER: Dear God, forgive me for sustaining anger,
disappointment, and frustration. Help me to spend more
time searching for ways to reconcile myself with others

and to eliminate the thoughts which keep me apart from them. In Your name, I search for peace. Amen.

3
Thoughts on a Dreary Day

A wet, cool, rainy day causes all kinds of personality changes in people. Some become depressed or bored; others feel a comfortable coziness. Still others accept rainy days as their forte, experiencing a joy in working.

Mostly, our moods on rainy days are self-developed or are reactions to personal experiences. Someone who lives in a rainy climate might say, "Just another rainy day." The person who lives in a hot, dry climate might shout out with enthusiasm, "Glory to God, it's raining!"

Normally, rain or snow places restrictions on us which we could do without—limiting our activities to indoors, or having to bundle up to do whatever must be done outdoors.

Having to confine our activities indoors is a chance to remind ourselves that the mind is a wonderful gift. Our minds can provide us with entertainment and activity which can temporarily shut out the restrictions from the weather and difficulties we may be having. A lively and interesting discussion over lunch while the elements howl outside can be wonderfully stimulating and refreshing.

On the morning I write this I was awakened to a cold

and cloudy, misty day. The crows were cawing. Listening to them took my mind back to the days when my grand-parents lived on a farm in an isolated section of southern Oklahoma. I remember vividly when my sister and I were very young and we would lie warm and comfortable in Grandma's heavy goose-feather bed, her colorful patch-work quilt as a cover.

Our experiences, especially the ones we enjoyed the most, can be filed into our amazing craniums for instant recall. We experience again the feelings and comfort they brought.

God gave each of us a mind to use. Exercising the mind can give us the greatest possible joy. Not using the mind is an affront to our Maker.

PRAYER: Dear God, thank You for that wonderful thing called the brain. It rescues us from boredom, gives us creative ability, and provides a way of thinking through our rainy days. Help us use our minds efficiently and generously for the benefit of ourselves and for man-kind in Your name. Amen.

4
Office Changes

Everyone experiences changes. Changes come by choice, by new circumstances, or by force from others. When it comes in the office, the immediate response is usually, "What did I do wrong?" A feeling of insecurity raises its frightening head.

Most changes in the office are not directed at anyone or because anyone has done anything wrong. Management may have seen a gap in the assignment of responsibilities; or a job vacancy is anticipated; or management wants to try a different emphasis; or promotions are in order; or the acceptance of different responsibilities for that department is being planned; or management wants to experiment with what they see as a better mix of talents and abilities.

The introduction of new office procedures or equipment may simply be a call for a remix of employee talents.

The biggest shock and resistance to change comes from employees who do not know ahead of time that the change is coming and who are not being told the reasons or not being asked to become a part of the decision-making process. These are management responsibilities and should be addressed by management and employees together.

But changes there will be, regardless of how they are carried out or how brutally they may be imposed. One day you are doing one thing, the next day something different, possibly without meaningful explanation and with shocking suddenness.

Jesus' disciples experienced shocking changes in their lives. They were called to serve with Him, sometimes without even the chance to say good-bye to family and friends.

But because they readily accepted the call, they became vital participants in one of the greatest revelations to mankind. Called from being tentmakers, physicians, fishermen, tax collectors, and other occupations, the disciples discovered they were being called to do more important things.

The ultimate shock came when Jesus was crucified.

Although the changes in our own lives are not often very great, we can turn those changes into valuable assets by the way we accept them.

The person who blows his top the instant the boss announces changes in office assignments is not giving the change a fair chance. Time is needed to experience the change and the new circumstances surrounding that change.

Time is needed for reassessment, to compare the new responsibilities with personal talents and desires. To automatically nurse alienated feelings can short-circuit what may eventually turn out to be change for the best. Emotional blowups seldom result in positive gains, and probably will damage the status quo of desirable situations.

If, after a fair period of time and evaluation, a change seems to be a backward step, there are avenues of escape. A change of jobs and companies may be needed. Life goals may need adjusting. Simply hanging in there to await what happens next may be best.

Any decision must take into account the important obligations each of us has assumed—to family, to lifelong goals, to religious faith, to self. All this takes time for our human minds to absorb and assess thoroughly.

The disciples often had second thoughts about the changes in their lives. Ultimately they sought advice from God, as revealed to them by Jesus.

Shouldn't we, too?

PRAYER: God of change and reconciliation, help us to look forward. Grant that we can anticipate change when possible, and soften our reaction to change when it bursts unexpectedly upon our lives. May we see the advantages of change, as well as the disadvantages, and visualize the doors of opportunity which have been left ajar. Amen.

5
Reasoning It Out

How human beings use their reasoning power to make decisions is a fascinating study.

There is the joke about the man who was indignant when the bank sent him a notice that his checking account was overdrawn. The man went to the bank and complained, saying the account could not possibly be overdrawn since he still had some blank checks left.

That humorous demonstration of flawed reasoning, unfortunately, is all too true even when we think we are being rational in making serious and important decisions affecting our personal lives.

Information used in reasoning is not always verified, and false weight is sometimes given to information which may be dependable. The result is sometimes disastrous when the hard facts of reality hit.

Learning to reason is not difficult. But it does take conscious effort to instill learning to reason as a habit.

People who become adept at reasoning are able to live

happier and more efficient lives without dawdling over
matters that may not be very important. They are able to
make better and faster decisions and avoid many of life's
pitfalls.

Political and religious demigods attain followings
through false reasoning, presenting "facts" which look
good at first glance but are difficult to untangle later.

Jesus taught with reasoning power through parables
and examples. He taught that it is worth abandoning all
else in order to seek the really important things in life.
The parables of the lost coin, the lost sheep, and the trea-
sure found in a field are His examples of how to keep in
mind the true value of the kingdom of God.

To put personal reasoning powers to work, three major
steps must be taken:

(1) Doublecheck the facts needed by using more than
one source which is considered dependable.

(2) Weigh the significant disadvantages of each path
which might be taken.

(3) Weigh the worthwhile advantages of each path
which might be taken.

Write down the facts on paper. List the disadvantages
and advantages of each possibility, placing them in sepa-
rate columns so they can be compared side by side.

Fix the goal in your mind and all the good and bad
points involved in attaining that goal. Pray about it. Then
lay all thoughts of it aside for a few days, or at least a few
hours. Let the mind reason for a while on its own without
interference. When you do go back to the problem, you'll
often find the obvious decision sitting there ready to be
picked. If not, go through the process again.

This is one of the reasons why Jesus often went away by

Himself to pray. He sought the time and prayer He knew was needed to make honest appraisal and come to proper and correct decisions through His God-given reasoning powers.

Each of us needs contemplative prayer time to help in making significant decisions.

When George Nigh was governor of Oklahoma he was criticized for what some people thought was slowness in coming to decisions concerning state government problems. Nigh said the time he used to make important decisions was positive and deliberate. He said he would rather take the time to make a right decision than hurry up the process and regret it later.

Rational reasoning and decision making is needed within the Christian faith. Studying the Scriptures, using a good concordance and Bible commentary, praying, and leaning on a dependable friend help us develop the faith we need to reach dependable decisions.

PRAYER: Dear God, since I am human I know I will make mistakes. I pray that I will use to the best of my ability the reasoning and decision-making powers You have given me. I pray that I will be able to understand all sides in any decision I make and then choose what is best with Your help. Amen.

6
Blah Days Are Launching Pads

There are days when these bodies of ours are not up to par. We're not sick, but we feel as if we are coasting along out of gear. Our bodies do not always respond or feel the vigor and eagerness we would like.

When we feel this way at work, it can affect the quality of our production and our relationships with friends and co-workers in ways we don't like. We snap back at people when we think they are being too pushy. We find ourselves strangely wishing that even our friends would leave us alone. We are afraid we might say something we wish we hadn't.

We wish we could take off and go tramping through the woods with a sack lunch. Or we may simply want some uninterrupted time to enjoy a favorite piece of music.

How can we handle our days of blah?

The first step is to acknowledge that those days will come occasionally, probably in spite of anything we can do to head them off. We can become so comfortable with them in a world of hyperactivity that they are welcomed. Yet we need to respond to the blahs before they become too embedded in our lives and control too much of our personality.

It is one thing to give in to the blahs and something else to let that feeling go outside ourselves and affect our relationships with others. It will take conscious effort to put the reins, bridle, and bit on our galloping outward reactions. We may need to pause and think a bit longer about our responses to others so we do not overreact.

Simply to realize that we may be reacting to something that normally we wouldn't give a second thought to is to win most of the battle. One way to help ourselves is to remember that overreacting to something makes us feel worse afterward and places on us the extra burden of having to make up for the damage.

The more experienced I get in this thing called living, the more I discover there are certain thoughts or actions I can call up which override or cancel my below-par feelings.

One trick is to carry out some little pleasant surprise for someone else. Inviting someone to eat lunch with me or complimenting someone on a job well done seems to pull my mind away from the blahs.

Another thing to realize is that others in the office may be having their own blah day. This is an opportunity to do for them what you would want someone to do for you. A quick compliment or a positive word may be called for. Sometimes simply leaving them alone without our constant prattle would be the very thing they welcome.

Positiveness in our lives is an active, vital force. To use it to the advantage of our friends and neighbors, as well as of ourselves, is to live Christianity in the fullest sense.

PRAYER: Dear God, how grateful we are that You have not made us as machines which hum along unfeeling and dull until they break. Thank You for high days, low days, blah days—and the ability to do something about them or simply wait them out with patience. With the strength and abilities You have given us and renew in us daily, we realize that the only constant in our lives is change. Thank You for life. Amen.

7
The Worth of Christians

I recently read a statement of faith that I like very much, affirming the worth of all God's children. During times of stress, particularly those induced by others, it is helpful to remember that all who have called upon His name and believed in Him are His. The statement reads in part: "I believe in God who created woman and man in God's own image, who created the world and gave both sexes the care of the earth. . . . I believe in the wholeness of the Savior in whom there is neither Jew nor Greek, slave nor free, male nor female, for we are all one in salvation."

God lifts each of us to the highest possible level. We are all glorified equally in His grace.

PRAYER: Thank You, God, for refusing to make any one of us second class. We follow with gratitude Your design of our character, our abilities, our vulnerabilities. We are grateful for the power of Your strength and encouragement and for the fact that each of us can reach to the highest of our potential with Your blessing. Amen.

8
Overcoming Anger

When tension in the office has boiled to the explosion point and you feel yourself going out of control, it is probably already too late to head off disaster. Conflict, whether verbal or physical, is one human feeling which is best dealt with *before* an incident arises, whenever possible. An angry person at the explosion point cannot see the other side's viewpoint. The results can be disastrous on friendships and job.

Beliefs leading to anger and conflict always have two or more sides, even though under more rational circumstances some of those sides may not be backed up with facts. The key word is *belief*.

An employee may think the boss is all wet—and maybe he is. On the other side, the boss may think the employee is unreasonable and irrational. The boss may also think the office would operate more efficiently if the angry employee would seek a job elsewhere.

In truth, the one who may let his anger get away from him is really the one most able to regain control. That person has it within his power to stop the anger before it turns into conflict.

In an article in the *Kiwanis* Magazine, October 1985, Jane Murray Alexander writes about four positive steps which can be taken to ease explosive feelings and turn life into a richer, more fun-filled experience.

Her suggestions are:

1. Evaluate the difference between acknowledging anger and acting it out. If you feel a strong, blood-boiling desire to take action, cool it long enough to think through an alternative positive reaction.

2. Evaluate each situation individually before taking action. You don't want to be a doormat, but you don't want to be a bully, either. Conflicts with others in the office come in varying degrees, some requiring firmness, others compromise, others an ultimatum, and still others an apology.

3. Use techniques for dissolving the urge to make physical response to anger. Try exercise or a fast walk in the fresh air, alone, where there are no rules and no competition.

4. Change your thinking. Only you can do that. You can't change the thinking of others very well. You can change your inner and outer responses, which no one else can do for you.

Although human beings are creatures of habit, they are not preprogrammed computers, unable to change.

I would add another tactic. Go sit in your car or any place you can be alone for five minutes. Breathe deeply and exhale slowly, relaxing all your muscles. Close your eyes and say a prayer, seeking strength to change tactics. The main thing is to get past the immediate difficult moment so you can look at the situation rationally.

If you can't think of words to pray, say the Lord's Prayer to yourself. There are plenty of words, thoughts, and ideas in that one prayer to guide your mind and spirit into something more manageable. Say the Lord's Prayer again, slowly. You'll find the potential conflict getting smaller, shrinking as a deflating balloon.

This is the power of prayer. It works.

PRAYER: "Our Father, who art in heaven, Hallowed be thy name. Thy kingdom come, Thy will be done, On earth as it is in heaven. Give us this day our daily bread; And forgive us our debts, As we have forgiven our debtors; And lead us not into temptation, But deliver us from evil" (Matt. 6:9-13, RSV).

9
Priorities

I once saw a wooden toy which, when a blue button was punched, popped up a red button. If a child punched the red button, the white button popped up, and so on. A very small child can laugh and giggle for several minutes over punching the buttons and watching others pop up. No matter how fast and how hard the child works, other buttons always appear, waiting to be punched.

As a game, the toy is a fun diversion. We often find the same kind of situation in real life. No matter how hard and long we work, there is always something else to do next. If several next things to be done are equally important, a decision must be made. Add to this the strong, driving desire to get ahead and get things done as soon as possible, and tension appears. Too much tension is damaging to our health.

Dr. William J. Diehm, a clinical psychologist, says that people sometimes get their priorities out of order without realizing it. Some women who are eager to please their bosses put their careers ahead of their husbands and families. Husbands often do the same thing.

The signal which comes out of such a situation is that the spouse, children, other members of the immediate family, and even friends get the idea that the career is all that matters.

I'm not advocating that people who have families must abandon careers or job opportunities. It happens occasionally that any career or job requires extra work and time for special projects, emergency situations, or situations which are not normal.

A business friend of mine once said that if a business continually demands an overdemanding work load, even for a normal work day, then something is wrong. If you find yourself having to choose between career and family and friends, the business is becoming a failure or the management isn't managing very well. Employees who find themselves working to tremendous excess year after year may be doing a lot of worthless things and going through lost motions.

Diehm makes these suggestions:

—Slow down. The quality of your work will probably improve and you can work more efficiently.

—Don't worry about not getting everything done everyday. Eliminating the worry probably means you'll get the work done sooner.

—Allow for mistakes. Take the time to correct them; or, if they cannot be corrected, make a note of the errors, notify someone if that is required, and forget them. Go on with the work.

—Delegate responsibility when possible.

—Be content with what can be done most efficiently.

—Most important, get involved spiritually and keep a silent prayer going. Pray to keep your world of work and your private world in perspective.

Being conscious of the need to keep life in proper perspective will do much to make living, working, and enjoying family and friends more fun.

PRAYER: Thank goodness, dear God, not everyone is impressed with my ability to be overly busy and get huge amounts of work done. Help me to work at my most efficient pace and still have the time and energy left to enjoy spouse, family, friends, and hobbies. They, too, are precious. Amen.

10
Wishing You Were Somewhere Else

In the midst of a day when everyone in my office was bent over work at their desk or computer screen, a co-worker and I came to a brief breathing period at the same time. She put her elbows on the desk, rested her chin in her hands, and looked straight at me to stress the seriousness of what she was going to say.

"Right now I'd give almost anything to be a clerk behind a jewelry counter," she said with a faint smile. I knew what she meant.

She is a good reporter. One of the best. She was covering city hall at the time and the involvement of her stories was complicated and incredibly detailed, but factual, complete, and understandable. It took long periods of concentration and all the experience she could muster to convert the mass of information coming out of city offices, council meetings, planning commissions, and budget sessions into news stories which the newspaper reader could digest and understand.

Her sense of news judgment required that she pick and choose information which mattered and that which did not. She knew that whatever she did, it would be right for some readers and wrong for others. But it was a part of the game of reporting in order to keep the public informed.

What she was doing came after hours of attending meetings and interviewing, taking copious notes. She also had to go through stacks of official reports and recommendations, choosing what she had time to read and leaving much of it for possible study later.

On top of all this, editors at nearby desks often interrupted her work wanting to know when stories would be ready.

The brief respite between the completion of one story and the beginning of the next prompted the head support and a desire to be doing something else.

To be fair, the jewelry-store clerk may be feeling the same way when a shopping rush is on, a slow customer holds up a line of people ready to make purchases, and the department head interrupts to say that the entire showcase must be changed. She may wonder why she didn't take up newspaper reporting.

We all get these feelings occasionally, regardless of what we may do for a living or how much we may normally enjoy what we do. When the hard times come we feel exposed, as if all our personal weaknesses were hanging out for all to see. We become drained physically and mentally.

The saving thought in all this is the joy of doing a good job in spite of the pressures. What is important is how well we serve others in their needs, whether our service be providing information or a product.

The fact that we can put our elbows on the desk and take even a small break serves as a relief from the pressure. It is what Jesus did when He pulled away from the crowd to rest and pray and ask for a moment of mental and spiritual relief.

Such moments are among the real little treasures of our lives which no one take from us.

PRAYER: Thank You, God, for providing me with the ability to make calm reflection in the midst of all this mess. The renewal of my strength, my interest in what I am doing, and the remembrance of my life goals make it fun again to keep at it. Amen.

11
Pressure

Which group of words best describes the Christmas season for you?

Group 1: Shopping, spending, hurrying, eating, talking, going, coming, waiting, wrapping, opening, cleaning, cooking, driving, paying.

Group 2: Praying, hoping, loving, worshiping, serving, patience, choosing, trusting, listening, sharing.

Is the pressure on or off for you during this season?

Which is more in keeping with God's Word?

Read Luke 10:38-42.

PRAYER: So many times, dear Lord, I do not take time to enjoy the season. Such enjoyment gets in the way of things I feel I must do. Stopping long enough to pray this prayer may redirect me, I pray, so that I create less pressure and more adoration of what You have wrought. Amen.

12
Changing Streams

As it does for many, the time may come when you realize you would rather be doing something else with your life.

The job you've been doing for several years may no longer be the challenge it once was. You're not tired of work, or dedication, or enthusiasm. You simply visualize something more interesting, more challenging, more fun, more beneficial—something more in keeping, for instance, with your growing Christianity along the road of life.

You'll never be able to make the change unless you start somewhere, sometime. You must be willing to sacrifice and work toward it. The change need not be so sudden and dramatic that the family income is shattered and you wonder where the next meal is coming from. But sacrifice there will be.

When I decided that publishing a small community weekly newspaper was turning out to be something of a dead-end career, I put my eyes on a goal of teaching at the college level. I managed to get a job teaching one class in photojournalism at a nearby university. Then I entered a master's degree program at another university which required part-time study on campus, but allowed most of the work to be done on the student's own. It was designed for people returning to the campus after many years, who had responsibilities of families and jobs.

I had to carefully juggle time, giving all I could to the teaching and degree study and cutting what I could out of running the newspaper and being with family. It was difficult, and sometimes I thought it was foolish. But after the goals were reached, I had a tremendous satisfaction that all the work had been worthwhile.

Susan Foster Ambrose, a health and psychology writer, said there are five steps which are helpful:

1. Decide what it is you want to accomplish, ignoring for the moment any practical obstacles.

2. Tell someone who can share and be enthused with you about your ideas.

3. Brainstorm on your own and with others you respect to learn how your desire can be accomplished.

4. Start getting involved. Enroll in a class for training you may need. Talk to people in the field, asking them how they got started. Especially talk to people who entered the work by switching from something else.

5. Set some goals, but realize that those goals might change, or be delayed, or even dropped if a better goal is found.[1]

The main point is to begin. Make a first step which you can handle without much risk, or that you can abandon with little damage if you change your mind. Then take another step, modifying your plans as you go, if needed. Keep at it.

Paul said in his Letter to the Philippians, "I press on toward the goal for the prize of the upward call of God in Christ Jesus. Let those of us who are mature be thus minded" (Phil. 3:14-15).

PRAYER: All my strength and confidence come from You, dear God. I have no other source to face the challenge I am seeking. Change of my life-style is so frightening. Yet I know that with Your help, with Your strength enfolding me, I can reach the goal I seek for a more fruitful perspective. Be with me now as I take one step at a time. Strengthen me where I am doing it right; give me pause and patience when I need to think things through a bit more. I put my trust in Your hands. Amen.

Note

1. Barbara Sher, *Wishcraft: How to Get What You Really Want* (New York: Ballantine, 1983).

13
Ask Yourself Why You Rush

As with Martha, who fretted over Mary's apparent unconcern about helping to serve the dinner (Luke 10:38-42), sometimes we rush around and do not realize what we are doing to ourselves and to others, and for what selfish reason.

You may ask yourself, "Why do I feel guilty when I take a minute at a break point in my work to stare out the window?"

If you are like many of us, you feel most comfortable under the boss's eyes while working at breakneck speed and under full load. However, no one can work at optimum efficiency for any great length of time. We are imperfect human beings.

A person works best at his most efficient level, not at his highest speed. The most comfortable and most efficient work level may be at a varied pace spiked with occasional rest periods.

So why the guilt?

There should be none if we are honest with the job, ourselves, the boss, and others working around us. The guilt may arise because we have mistakenly felt we need to prove something. Maybe we did not give our finest effort to some past project. Maybe we want to show up a fellow worker.

Jealousy, a feeling of inadequacy, and guilt are terrible things to live with. Throw them out along with the trash on your desk. Install whatever outlook might be needed to make your work most efficient and enjoyable.

PRAYER: "For thy name's sake, O Lord, pardon my guilt" (Ps. 25:11).

14
How Long, O Lord?

There is a beautiful song which the choir at our church sings occasionally: "How Long, O Lord?" The message which comes to me is that man's impatience is not a virtue. Patience is.

Whenever I buy something I want or need, I tend to be

impulsive during the shopping and purchase. I am not one to go trudging from one store to another, getting in and out of the car at a dozen parking lots, and then returning to the best deal. The first store I visit tends to have the best deal for me if they have an item similar to what I want.

Others I know, including my wife, Helen, can shop all day and still not find exactly the right thing. She has much more patience than I.

When working for a company, how long can you justify waiting for a raise in salary, a promotion, an office of your own, better equipment, or whatever you feel you need?

I was asked once by a "higher up" what it would take to make my work more valuable and more fulfilling to customers. He wanted a written report on my ideas. My enthusiasm soared. I thought it was my chance to have meaningful influence and to see some of my ideas incorporated into the work I was doing.

I worked on that report for several days and turned in several neatly typed pages. As I handed it in, the department head smiled and said he would read it over, but for me not to expect any changes soon. That was several years ago and nothing has come of the report. A downturn in the economy probably was the key factor. This expereince was, and still is, a disappointment.

I realize now that I had little patience with the possible success of that report. My spirits soared with hope, then gradually deteriorated. Now, my hard work and insight has almost been forgotten as it gathers dust in some file.

Ezekiel, the prophet for the exiled Jews, was told by God to preach the truth regardless of whether anyone paid any attention to him. The implication was that God knew Ezekiel would eventually be vindicated, even if that time came long after Ezekiel was dead and forgotten.

We cannot always force others or situations to do our bidding. Other people and various situations have minds of their own and may or may not pay attention. Our job is to do what is right, regardless of what others may do. God does not allow us to lord it over others, only over ourselves.

Patience is our friend. Without patience we can become frustrated, depressed, lose hope, and even go mad. With patience we can follow through the rough spots and eventually reach victory for a life which God intended us to have.

PRAYER: Dear God, we love the passage where Paul tells us in his letter to the church at Galatia that patience is a virtue along with love, joy, peace, and kindness. But it is a difficult thing to think of waiting as an asset. Open our eyes to patience and the realization that God's schedule is not necessarily our schedule. With patience, we pray to You. Amen.

15
Franticism

Overly busy days cannot overwhelm us unless we let them. The mental and spiritual capacities which God has given us are made to come to our rescue whenever we face a frantic schedule which threatens to destroy us.

A much-too-busy schedule on any particular day is something that happens to everyone from time to time. It makes no difference what the job is, things tend to pile up occasionally.

When it happens, we feel sorry for ourselves. We are convinced no one else really understands how over-worked we are—especially the boss. Yet, the work must be done and we must get with it even when we are convinced there is no hope for completing all the tasks on our schedule.

I can remember quite well one particular day. I had a horrible schedule. It was on a Monday, naturally. Several interviews had somehow piled up on the same day, it was the deadline day for several feature stories, only one of which had been written, and the news desk was expecting a log of stories for a special youth page which I had not completed.

In addition, I was supposed to pick up a couple of pairs of trousers which had been left at a store for altering; my watch had stopped running and needed a battery; a civic club meeting was scheduled at 6 PM, and the car badly needed servicing. When I went to the parking garage to drive to the first interview, I saw an ominous puddle of water underneath the radiator. Getting that fixed meant somehow getting the car to the garage so I could get it back the next day.

I became so wrought up that I became virtually incapable of operating rationally. I broke out in a cold sweat. My hands were shaking and my vision blurred. I sat down in the car, determined to take a few valuable minutes to get hold of myself. Something had to give. *There is only so much a human being can take,* I said to myself.

But all I could think about was the time ticking away. I felt a sense of panic arising from deep inside. I made another vow that something had to be done and it had to be done now.

Since that day I have learned several things. One is to watch the schedule in advance. I have learned to say no with a firmness which surprises me even yet. I even say no when I know I don't have a thing planned, because I realize my need to have room to think and plan.

Most importantly, I have learned to place a priority on matters, doing first things first. I had to learn to handle the important things and delay the other things, or forget them entirely. It no longer bothers me to call up and cancel or postpone activities I don't have time for.

The familiar story of Martha and Mary when Jesus visited them in their home is as valuable as always. Martha, you remember, was busy fixing the dinner, trying to get things ready for an enjoyable meal with their guests. Mary, sensing a strong need to be with and learn from Jesus, stayed to talk with Him, passing up helping with the preparations.

Martha complained. Jesus admonished her, saying that Mary had found the important thing to do.

We need that advice in an age which seems to stimulate and motivate people beyond reason. What is important? What is not important? What can be put off and done later? What needs to be done now? We must choose, even if arbitrarily, to keep our sanity, to keep our mental capacities and our spirits intact.

If we do not, we can rightly be accused of abusing the powers and capacities God has so wonderfully given us. We will be held accountable. We are continually being tested on how we handle our human capabilities.

God is always with us when we need Him. Yet, He does not expect us to abuse the gift of life. Caring for ourselves is a part of the responsibility God has given to us along with our freedom. We are free to accept or reject God.

Still, we will be held accountable.

PRAYER: Oh, God, who has infinite patience with me and who never gives me more to do than I can handle, teach me to be better to myself. Teach me that being frantic over too many things is not the life You gave me. Calming my troubled soul is as simple as stopping and listening to Your assurance. Amen.

16
Revenge

Any time you register a complaint, there is always the chance of sparking revenge.

It matters not what the complaint is or who or what the complaint is directed against. If your words hit a sensitive spot or a revengeful person, you can anticipate a reaction.

Luckily for our tender feelings and bodies, most revenge tends to be temperate and does not find physical expression.

If the revengeful feelings of the other person build up particularly fast and strong, the reaction is more likely to be expressed quickly and strongly. You are likely to feel it on the bounce in the form of strong words or a fist in the teeth.

The longer a feeling of revenge is subdued, the weaker its expression—normally. Some, however, let hard feelings fester and develop until they explode at some later date. Then there are people who are as angels who have no feelings of revenge regardless of the complaints.

Actually, the chance of revenge or backlash may be quite remote considering how infrequently people are beaten over the head with angry words.

Once, when I complained about something an editor did to a story I had painstakingly spent hours writing, the revenge taken was silence. The editor pointedly ignored me, even when we were in small-group conversations.

Gradually, the hard feelings subsided, but I still get the distinct message that I am not one of that editor's favorite people.

The best defense against possible revenge is openness and friendship. Talk to the other person as a friend. Apologize if you discover you were wrong to complain, but stick to your guns if you know you are right. Make it clear there are no hard feelings and you want the friendship to survive intact.

This can be hard work. Any friendship worth keeping is hard work.

A passage in Psalms, I think, makes an appropriate personal prayer when we are subjected to retribution:

PRAYER: "Be gracious to me, O Lord! Behold what I suffer from those who hate me" (Ps. 9:13).

17
Euphoria

Euphoria is a word not used very often. It means happiness to the point of jubilation, a healthy feeling of well-being or elation. It is that feeling when you want to kick up your heels, when you feel you could fly without wings, and make a huge success of anything you might want to tackle. It is a feeling I have today as I write this, a day of warm sun, relaxed mental state, and a jillion things I would like to do.

Such a feeling, as much as we enjoy it and look forward to it occasionally, also is unreal, sometimes misleading. It can get us into trouble if we don't keep our heads.

Euphoria, or giddy happiness, doesn't last very long. It continues only as long as we are willing to wallow in it selfishly. The feeling can cover up or cause us to ignore the needs of others who are nearby or who are dear to us. Others may feel left out, getting the feeling that you are showing your real self and that self doesn't include them.

While a person is enjoying euphoria, he is more likely than usual to do something crazy or ill-advised which will be regretted later. When the letdown comes, the regretted action will loom larger than life and the letdown multiplies. We wonder how in the world we could have done such a nutty thing.

Yet, happy exuberance is not something to be ashamed

of, so long as the source of the happiness is not over tri-
flings, or is not at the expense of someone else's
happiness.

A writer in the Psalms defines someone who has godly
happiness as one who has hope in God, who executes justice for the oppressed and who gives food to the hungry
(Ps.146:5-7, RSV).

Paul writes in Romans that happiness is freedom in
God without self-incrimination, that such happiness is to
be kept to self to avoiding damaging the faith of those who
are not yet emancipated (Rom. 14:22).

Paul was thinking that those who had fully accepted
God would know that it is not necessary to observe little
details of the Hebrew law, such as what to eat and what to
wear. The important thing is to love each other, to love
justice, to care for the sick and hurting and hungry.

But he warned it would be damaging to many people's
infantile budding faith to go about telling them they can
forget the law. Some would feel that since they don't need
to observe the law, they don't need to observe much of
anything.

James provides yet another aspect of happiness: Steadfastness (Jas. 5:11).

Standing for what is right in the sight of God, regardless of the consequences, makes a man happy in the long
run. Such things as honesty, refusal to use others as personal stepping stones, and all the other assets connected
with loving our neighbors contributes to man's happiness
if practiced with steadfastness.

So, what are the scriptural writers telling us?

Euphoria, the joy that knows no bounds, is a positive
part of life to be enjoyed. But it should be reserved for

things of importance. Being able to buy a new television set or a new car or a fur coat are not to be compared with comforting the hurting, feeding the hungry, and seeking justice for the downtrodden.

PRAYER: Thank You, God, for the boundless joy I feel in Your big wonderful world. I must be nearer to You when I feel that way. Help me to channel that joy, that feeling of being able to tackle anything, in a way which will also spread that joy to others. Amen.

18
Who Bugs You?

Is there someone in your office who gives you the shivers and shakes every time that person walks in? I had an editor once to whom I reacted that way.

It seemed that on every day when I had a long list of things to do and everything was on a tight schedule, he would demand I drop everything to do some project he had in mind.

I resented that he never asked what I was doing or never put himself into the position of having to judge whether what he wanted done and what I was already committed to do was the more urgent.

More often than I like to remember, I would be forced to call people back, canceling or postponing interviews and having to explain why I couldn't come to this or that meeting.

As long as he was in the room, I worked with a tenseness I didn't need, wondering when he was going to step my way and make a mess of my carefullylaid schedule.

This kind of situation is a difficult thing to handle. But sometimes it can be done by working your way carefully and confidently into the problem.

One of the main goals is to gain the confidence of whoever is bugging you. Make it a point every day to be friendly. Drink coffee together, eat lunch together occasionally. Let that person know of some of the projects and ideas you are working on, including the ones you are initiating yourself as well as assignments you have been given.

You may be surprised how much help that person may give you in realizing successful completion of your own projects. More important, the other person cannot help but be more sympathetic when a request is made and you explain you are already booked on an important project for that particular time span. Together you can decide which is more important at the time.

Be willing to negotiate. Possibly you can sense that whatever it is you are being asked to do can be done at a different time, saving your own carefully-laid plans. Or, possibly your own plans can be delayed without undue hardship.

You should keep in mind that when someone else, especially a supervisor or boss, asks you to do something, it could be an important matter which only you can be trusted to do properly. That is an honor which should be taken at face value.

The important thing is to aim at working WITH people, not against or for people.

PRAYER: Dear God, I sometimes let resentment against certain individuals build up inside me, forgetting that You love them, too. I forget that they have their own set of concerns, goals, and problems which concern You and should concern me, too. Go with me now into my new day of work, remembering that everyone should be my friend who is a friend of Yours. Amen.

19
It's Only an Apparition

Understanding what co-workers around us are going through can help us to understand some of the mysterious unexplainable things people do. We do not always know about the pressures, anxieties, and fears of others.

A reporter in the newsroom who had temporarily filled in for an editor who was on maternity leave, had an interesting observation upon returning to reporting work.

"She (the editor) always seems so calm," the reporter said. "Even with a heavy work load, she manages to be friendly with others, acting as if there was no stress or strain. While I was doing her job, I was under continual tension and considerable strain. I don't see how she does it."

I had to smile. Her comment brought back some fond, yet painful, memories of my days as publisher and editor of a hometown newspaper. After I had been operating the newspaper for about a year, one of the former owners stopped me on the street.

"You make it seem so easy," he said in admiration. I was honestly surprised at his comment. In my own mind I was going through mental and emotional anguish trying to grasp all the mechanics of running a newspaper, managing people, balancing the books, and the other many details as a newcomer to the entrepreneur scene.

Even when outwardly a person seems hypertensive, or there are bursts of temper and general crabbiness, appearances do not always relay truth. He may have personal problems which would be overwhelming if they were our own. Behind the surface appearance of the fellow worker who seems to be lazy or nonchalant about his job, there may actually be a beehive of nervous energy.

Over the years, every person manages to develop a certain amount of acting ability to mask inside turmoil or problems. Famous actors, actresses, and other performers attract audiences largely on the basis of the characterizations they portray. In real life they are about like the rest of us. Sometimes they are revealed in their private world as persons who have sunk into a pit of alcoholism or drugs. On the other hand, they may be wonderful people who have real concern over others and make wonderful personal friends.

We are so easily misled. John, the aged, last remaining disciple of Jesus, warned of deception.

"Beloved, we are God's children now; it does not yet appear what we shall be " (1 John 3:2).

And, in 2 John, verse 7, he says, "For many deceivers have gone out into the world, men who will not acknowledge the coming of Jesus Christ in the flesh; such a one is the deceiver and the antichrist."

John said Jesus risked, and preferred us to risk, intimacy with others. Those who act out an impression as a mask for their real feelings cannot risk intimacy.

There is a need for each of us to look inward to detect not only the deception we try to impose on others, but the deception with which we deceive ourselves.

What John seems to be saying is that we need to use our God-given brains to prevent or weed out the deception we practice. We need to admit that we do not always know what goes on in the minds and spirits of others, or even ourselves.

Knowing that, we can be more honest and caring for each other, traits which Jesus constantly demonstrated as worthy examples for our lives.

PRAYER: Oh, God, I continually portray to others what I am not. I cover up my bad habits instead of correcting them. I put up a false front in order to convey what I think others expect of me instead of living my own precious character which God has given me. May I carefully investigate my life, portraying what is real and good, changing what is bad, but forever being honest. Amen.

20
Mistaeks

Mistakes are the hidden snakes on the road to the success of any given day. No one can get entirely rid of the snakes. Throwing temper tantrums or ruining a perfectly good friendship because of mistakes only feeds more snake poison into the psyche. At best, all we can do is to observe preventive measures and take the appropriate serum when bitten.

There are positive steps to be taken:

—Correct mistakes as soon as and as best as possible. Warn others if they are involved or might be misled by the mistake.

—Look carefully at the situation to understand how the mistake was made and what might be done to prevent a recurrence.

—Don't dwell on mistakes unduly and don't expect never to make another. And, don't expect others working around you never to make mistakes, either.

—Once a mistake is acknowledged and everything has been done to correct it and to protect from a repeat performance, forget it and go on to other work.

—Do plow ahead, realizing that mistakes, snakes, and blue days are a part of life from which we can learn.

It is how we handle mistakes that counts.

PRAYER: Dear God, help us to keep our mistakes in perspective, realizing we are going to make more on some days than on other days. Occasionally, we will even make a whopper. We know, however, that You are always with us and that Your strength can flow through us to handle every situation if we only will let it. Amen.

21
Tension

A certain amount of tension is necessary for each of us to get going each day and maintain an eagerness about our work. An excess of tension which encompasses worry, anxiety, and apprehension can be damaging to our health.

Being overly tense sets the scene for mistakes, flaring tempers, high blood pressure, poor appetite, and a host of other problems. Fortunately, there are ways of controlling tension, even while sitting at your desk.

This method is taught by major health centers across the country:

—Sitting comfortably in a straight chair with hands hanging at your side, take a deep breath on a count of four seconds.

—Hold the breath in your lungs for four seconds, and then breathe out for four seconds, thinking of a relaxing word such as *peace, calm,* or another word of your choice. Close your eyes, if possible, or simply look blankly at some stationary object.

—Leave the lungs exhaled for four seconds; then repeat the process three or four times. Each time consciously let muscles relax by sections, beginning with neck and shoulders and gradually working down to legs and feet.

—Besides the physical relaxation, think on these words

from Paul, who was reflecting on what Jesus said many times and in many ways: "Have no anxiety about anything, but in everything by prayer and supplication with thanksgiving let your requests be made known to God. And the peace of God, which passes all understanding, will keep your hearts and your minds in Christ Jesus" (Phil. 4:6-7).

PRAYER: Amen.

22
Appreciating Help

Sometimes we do not realize or appreciate the work others do on our behalf. Only in some quiet moment, when we are left to think, it comes to us that so-and-so really went out of his or her way to do something nice for us.

Paul, in his letter to the church at Corinth, expressed thankfulness for Titus, whom he felt had the same earnest care for members of the church which Paul had.

The best time to thank someone is immediately after the good deed. But, if the good deed is realized hours or days or weeks later, there is still time.

A letter of appreciation, a friendly visit, a card, or a call are all appropriate responses, even when late.

Keeping the response in proper perspective is also important in order to convey sincerity. Overdone expressions of appreciation are an embarrassment. Underdone expressions hint of insincerity. A sincere conservatively done "thank you" is appreciated and lets the recipient know you care.

Paul, realizing that Titus would probably read or hear about Paul's letter to the Corinthians, was not only showing his faith in a friend, but showing appreciation to Titus.

Showing and expressing appreciation for what others contribute positively to our lives is a form of love. That's what our Christian faith is all about.

PRAYER: Help me, God, to be sensitive to those around me who care for others. Protect me from jealousy toward those who receive praise and recognition for their caring attitudes. Help me realize that caring for others contains its own reward, and my thanks to those who help me is recognition and acceptance of what Christ taught when He commanded us to love one another. Amen.

23
Future Shock Is Here Now

When Alvin Toffler's book, Future Shock, came off the press, people were amused, entertained, became fearful, or expressed considerable doubt about what Toffler was saying. Every age is a shock, producing fear and doubt in some— laughter in others.

What Toffler did was to put into words what he saw as the approaching drastic change in yet another age in our society

These changes in society are nothing new. The world has gone from the age of the hunter to the age of agriculture, to the age of industry, and now well into the age of information. There will be other ages to come as long as man occupies this planet.

These ages need not come as shocks.

Those who have faith in God know what is dependable, know what is the same from the distant past to the foreseeable future and beyond. Those of faith who see the changes going on around them may be amused, fascinated, or awed by those changes. But, they need not be shocked into paralyzing disbelief, inaction or withdrawal from the world.

What difference does it make, they can say, whether travel is in a bouncing stagecoach behind a team of stinky horses, or in a smooth and plush airliner high over cumulus clouds. The airline method of travel is much more comfortable, faster, convenient. But that doesn't change basic values of human relationships, honesty, justice, and caring for each other.

Some people appear to accept the changes in society but still look at those changes through eyes tuned to twenty, thirty, and fifty years ago. Some want to bring back the "good old days" which in many cases espoused values which were no more of God then than they are now.

In a sense, for those people, future shock is here now.

For those of faith who view the way we live, the way we survive, the way goods are manufactured, distributed, and bought, the clothes we wear, the foods we eat—they see it merely as a passing parade which has no permanent value.

PRAYER: God of the universe, of change, of justice, of love, forgive me for latching onto the things of no permanent value. May I fasten my guidelines to Your spirit which dwells within me. May I see through the glitter, the noise, the color of contemporary society to Your admonition for justice, for caring, for love of our fellow beings. Amen.

24
The Rhino Theory

We can stay out of a lot of trouble by living within a thick skin.

Words uttered by others in certain combinations or with certain emphasis, can sometimes penetrate a vulnerable spot to hit our temper trigger. We may react, without thinking, in a way we later regret bitterly.

Telling crude jokes, repeating rumors, spouting put downs, and laughing at the wrong things, are usually common commodities in the office. These are things no one seems to be able to control very well.

There are defenses and positive reactions which can be put into play.

Most unkind and hurtful comments can simply be ignored because they are unimportant. Such passing remarks are cast in ignorance or mistaken judgment and are not worth creating a scene. Ignoring such comments does not necessarily convey a neutral reaction. Pointedly ignoring something sends the signal that such expressions are not appreciated.

Developing a thick skin will lessen the hurt, even from deliberately cast hateful thoughts. An upbeat reaction can sometimes reduce outrageous comments to the silly level, and even produce a genuine love.

"You're a real turkey," one man said to an office co-worker after they had argued over a disagreement.

Smiling back, the victim disarmed the situation by readily agreeing. "It takes one to know one," he said. "I like my turkey slow baked with plenty of corn bread dressing and gravy. How about lunch?"

Crude jokes about ethnic minorities can lead to highly embarrassing situations.

One man I know never seemed to join in when degrading jokes were told on minorities. No one particularly noticed this for a long time. Until one day it was learned accidentally that the man's son-in-law was a member of a minority, who was highly admired and who had become a loving and loved member of the family.

Needless to say it suddenly became self-examination day for those who had told those endless ethnic jokes. Sadly, they realized they must have deeply hurt their friend many, many times.

God does not wish us to be dumb, but to use our minds, our spirit, and our compassion in dealing with others. The presence of degrading words in any conversation must be dealt with on both sides—the one speaking them to realize the damage being done and to seek forgiveness; and the victim to develop the hide of a rhinoceros and the ready ability to forgive.

PRAYER: Dear God, in my unthinking haste to criticize others unfairly, even in fun and misguided truth—and to react in anger too quickly when others do so—help me to deepen my understanding of caring for others. I pray I will be as gentle and forgiving of others as You are with me. Amen.

25
Witnessing on the Job

I saw two caterpillars crawling across my lawn the other day, chatting away and minding their own business. Suddenly a beautiful butterfly flew over them. As the caterpillars looked up, one of them nudged the other and said, "You couldn't get me up on one of those things for a million dollars."

We look at what others do, or see things we would like to do but are afraid to try, and say to ourselves, "We wouldn't do that for a million dollars." That is how many of us look at the prospect of testifying to our faith at work.

The thing which seems to bug us is the idea that to witness to our faith we must go up to a perfect stranger, boldly cite a biblical passage, and blurt out, "Brother, are you saved?" There are many effective ways of testifying to our faith in the office. Let us look at some suggested ways of conveying living testimonies to God:

CREATIVE LISTENING—Listen to the conversations of others around you. Praise their thinking when it fits into the mold of Christ. Listen to the complaining or hurting or confused co-worker who simply needs someone to bounce off their frustrations, fears, and loneliness. You are serving a real need when you do this and you don't have to say much of anything.

If someone needs to talk, but is hesitant to keep the conversation going, ask a carefully thought-out question that doesn't probe into privacy. Then listen. When they stop, ask another question, and then another, until they indicate they want to change the subject or end the conversation.

Make them your mentor, assuming that they are in control and you are the student. Everyone you meet knows more about some subject than you do.

TESTIFYING WITHOUT WORDS—Simply walking away from a bad situation speaks louder than any combination of words.

A man I had lunch with was known to have every prejudice in the book. Offensive nicknames for minorities sprinkled his conversation. A friend of mine who was also eating with us listened to this barrage of built-in hate for only a short period before he suddenly looked at his watch and remembered "a previously scheduled engagement." He picked up his check and headed for the cashier. Others in the group also got up to leave.

I don't know if the man with the offending speech caught on, but the incident was still a testimony.

MAKE FRIENDS WITH THE UNLOVABLE—This is difficult and sometimes seems to be a great waste of time. People who are difficult or have imposed on themselves some vow of isolation make it difficult to be around them. They may be afraid of other people because of some past unfortunate experience.

Nothing, however, is impossible with persistence and faith. A cheery "Hello" or "Good morning" or "See you in the morning" spoken every day over a period of many days can open a communication on which a conversation can begin.

The break may come when you find yourselves at coffee break alone.

BE GENUINELY INTERESTED IN OTHERS—Show real interest in what others are saying, even if they are a virtual rattlebrain. Somewhere among all those confusing words are thoughts worth hearing and understanding.

If the other person is closedmouthed, ask questions that have been sparked by your curiosity. Ask about their family, their hobbies, their previous jobs or about something you want to know on which they are knowledgeable. Unless there is genuine interest, which readily shows through in the tone of your voice and intensity of eye contact, you cannot develop the rapport for effective witnessing.

FORGIVENESS—Writing as a reporter for a large daily newspaper, I sometimes find myself angered over poor editing of stories I worked long, hard hours to research and write. Forgiveness is difficult and comes slowly. But with time and effort genuine forgiveness comes and friendships survive.

This is a responsibility which must be assumed if we are to witness for our faith.

DIRECT WITNESSING WITH WORDS—This is the most difficult of all. Most of us overuse words in such horrible, condescending, and arrogant ways. When did you

last back off from a group of people and listen to the overall babble?

We talk when we should be listening. We talk before
putting brain in gear. We make words cheap and unwanted by using so many of them to convey so little intelligence. We talk far beyond what anyone wants to hear.

We must learn to be careful with words, to make every
word count, to speak only after careful consideration of
the idea we want to convey. There is always a way to say
it better and with fewer attacks on the eardrums.

There are other tools in our arsenal of witnessing.

Referring people to sources of information or comfort
when we cannot furnish it ourselves.

Prayer.

Reading from the Bible.

Helping someone who has a difficult task.

Sharing sympathetically a difficult, unhappy or joyful
experience.

Being an example in the quality and dedication of our
work.

None of this is easy. Most of us must learn how to tes-
tify by little bits and pieces. It takes time to get the feel of
it and become comfortable with testifying, regardless of
the method used.

One other thing. Occasionally we must confront situations head on. We may rebel, thinking that Jesus did not
confront. But Jesus did confront. Read the first five
verses of chapter 3 in Mark. He confronted His accusers.
So must we on certain specific rare occasions and in a
Christlike way.

PRAYER: Dear God, realizing that to change my ways

and to adopt new techniques for following Christ, I must take one step at a time. As I learn to witness to others under the conditions of my life, encourage me, keep me within Your strength. Together we can witness to the Christ within others as well as to the Christ within me. Amen.

26
Striking Back

Everyone seems to have a breaking point. It comes when a persistent irritation finally overwhelms us and we get the urge to strike back.

I have seen normally sane people become so upset with the constant ringing of a telephone that they picked it up and threw it against the nearest wall.

What isn't so funny is when the irritant is another human being and the urge is to smash a fist into the guy's teeth. Jesus was asked about this.

He said we should forgive other people's trespasses upon us seventy times seven. That does not mean exactly 490 times, but forgiveness into infinity.

Paul also made it quite plain: "Put on then, as God's chosen ones, holy and beloved, compassion, kindness, lowliness, meekness, and patience, forbearing one another and, if one has a complaint against another, forgiving each other; as the Lord has forgiven you, so you also must forgive" (Col. 3:12-13).

I know a young man who is a regular motor mouth. Ask him a question and he answers, adding one postscript after another into the rest of the afternoon. It is difficult and irritating to put up with such a sticky conversationalist.

Actually there is no conversation, only him talking and others listening. He is utterly fascinated with his own voice.

So, what do we sufferers do? God has said we should put up with it, forbear, have compassion, and forgive.

PRAYER: Dear God, no one told me the Christian life would be easy. People who provoke me to the point of wanting to strike back are among those difficult for me to love. But You love them, I know. So I try. Amen.

27
The Whale Factor

All of us, at one time or another, have spouted off at someone else for their apparent stupidity. We feel terrible when we learn the other person was ill, experiencing grief, was distracted in some way, or—horrible of horrors—was right and we were wrong.

It is difficult for anyone to entirely escape stepping in advertently into such situations. But the chance for doing that can be lowered considerably by realizing ahead of time that people are people and they are going to occasionally goof up for a very good reason—or for no reason at all.

In some circles it is taught that to be a successful manager or boss requires that person to be hard-nosed and aloof, barking at everyone who gets out of line. In some specific situations with certain kinds of employees, that might be justified. It can never be used effectively as an overall plan of conduct for success.

The best boss I ever worked under was a lovable old man who was a friend to all. His employees would have done, and often did, back flips for him if he asked them to. The old man's business was one of the most successful in the state and one of the most respected. Few business organizations, even in today's high-tech, high-pressure atmosphere, can match it.

Empathetic and caring concern for each other, even when something goes wrong, is a gift of God. It works much better than grim impersonal fear where everyone blows up in everyone else's face.

PRAYER: Lord, help me to realize I am not the only one who has problems and that others may have better reason to be grumpy, hard to work with, or to pull stupid mistakes. And, God, when I arrive at a position of responsibility and leadership, help me to be evenhanded, compassionate, and understanding toward those I am assigned to supervise. In the name of the one who has love, compassion, and understanding for all of us all the time. Amen.

28
May I Interrupt You?

How do we react to interruptions?

That depends largely on what we are doing at the moment. If we are combing our hair and someone asks a question, we answer it and continue combing our hair. If we are concentrating on writing a sentence, as I am doing right now, and the telephone rings, we must leave a complicated thought process which is feeding on ideas and words stored up for immediate use.

In the first situation, it takes little brain power to comb our hair. We can continue doing that almost without thinking, while thinking about something else, or carrying on a conversation.

In the second situation, however, we have spent at least a little time loading up our immediate conscious brain with a reserve of information and proposed action which is needed to continue writing. An interruption of significance threatens to destroy some or all of that reserve which will require additional time to recreate, if we are able to do so at all.

A long, complicated interruption which requires the brain to take an entirely different direction and load up with information foreign to what was being done originally, makes it more difficult to return to the mental position we had when the interruption started. This kind of interruption is irritating and can even make a person angry.

As a writer in a busy newsroom, I have been interrupted as many as three or four times in the middle of composing one sentence. It is easy, under such circumstances to lose the entire thought process. Some people get the urge to throw something.

We can learn to anticipate interruptions and respond with a rational, Christian outlook. Believe it or not, we can even learn to make a positive experience out of interruptions.

It is most difficult to maintain a Christian perspective toward interruptions when they seem senseless or could have been avoided. However, if others have been interrupted in their work in order to come and interrupt us about something, they aren't worrying much about what the interruption might be doing to us. Somehow, maybe the fact they feel a bit of self-satisfying revenge in interrupting us, makes them feel better. So, we've made someone feel better and what's wrong with that?

Interruptions are a fact of life. All we can do is to soften their impact or make something positive out of them. They are simply there—like air, water, and coffee breaks.

What can we do?

To begin with, a working environment which produces too many interruptions is simply a poor working environment. The situation should be improved. There is a practical relationship between how frequently interruptions should be allowed and the quality of work to be expected. This is partly a management responsibility which may need prodding a bit. There may be a need for a telephone operator or a receptionist who can screen out at least some of the unnecessary interruptions.

Some kinds of work are insistently interruption prone, while other work is paced more leisurely with few detours. The aim here is to suggest attitudes and tactics which might reduce the mental devastation of interruptions on ourselves as well as others.

First, be conscious of the interruptions we inflict on others. When we feel a need to holler across the room to someone else who is deeply engrossed in some thought process—stop. Is the interruption really vital or is it merely convenient for you at that time? Could it just as easily be put off to a better time?

It also doesn't hurt if the telephone rings four or five times instead of just once. Give yourself time to get to a plateau or a natural breaking point before picking up the receiver. If you are lucky, someone else will answer it.

If an interruption comes from another person while you are in the middle of something you can't stop, hold up your hand signaling the other person to wait a minute. When you can turn loose, turn to the other person, smile, and give a greeting, letting them know you are ready to listen.

Some interruptions are opportunities to get acquainted with someone you'd like to meet. Maybe you need to take a break anyway.

Paul explained to the churches at Rome why he had not come to visit them earlier. It was due to the interruptions caused by the needs of Christians elsewhere. He simply told the truth.

"This is the reason why I have so often been hindered from coming to you," he said (see Rom. 15:22). Paul's words are a pattern we can use when interruptions delay our work and an explanation is called for.

PRAYER: Help me to realize my power of positive thinking, dear God, which allows me to take the little irritants of life and make something good from them. Amen.

29
Anticipation

Anticipation is one of the fun things. Anxiety is something we must put up with. People often get the two confused and vacillate from one to the other several times during the workday without separating the two very well.

An overdose of anxiousness can kill an otherwise joyful life. It can cause hypertension leading to a breakdown in mental and physical health.

Anticipation, on the other hand, produces a forward feeling of hope which has the capacity of making life happier and longer.

When we anticipate we usually know that something enjoyable is ahead although recognizing we may not know exactly what is going to happen. When we are anxious we also may know what's ahead and also recognize we may not know exactly what is going to happen, but we worry over what is expected of us and what dire consequences we will face.

Anticipation takes no particular preparation. We simply enjoy. With anxiousness, our faith is tested. If we have no faith we are left defenseless. With faith, anxiousness can be reduced to simply another interesting event in our lives.

"Have no anxiety about anything," Paul and Timothy write in Philippians 4:6 .

Anticipation, which is a form of hope, is endorsed in Galatians 5:5 when Paul writes, "We wait for the hope of righteousness."

Thus, there is a clear separation between the two feelings. They must be handled differently if we are to follow the teachings of Christ. Anxiety is tension and illness. Anticipation is an expectation of joy and life.

PRAYER: God, help me to anticipate and not be anxious. Forbid that I would become anxious over my anticipation, short-circuiting the strength of calm confidence which You offer to me. Amen.

30
Worry, Worry, Worry

Jesus went out of His way repeatedly to assure His listeners that there is no need to worry about our lives.

"Therefore do not be anxious about tomorrow, for tomorrow will be anxious for itself. Let the day's own trouble be sufficient for the day," He said (Matt. 6:34).

He said the same thing on specific subjects. We should not worry about what to eat, what to drink, what to wear, He said.

"And which of you by being anxious can add one cubit

to his span of life?"(v.27) Jesus asked. Indeed, medical science tells us that a continual diet of worry or anxiousness can bring on mental and physical illness.

So many of us live such uptight, frenzied, and hyperactive lives that we become flustered and somewhat confused when a delightfully enjoyable day comes along. We have never learned to relax and do nothing, or simply to let the joys of the day pull us along.

When the lead sheep jumps over a stick, members of the following flock also jump over the stick, even after the stick has been removed. When there is nothing to worry about, we humans continue to worry, making up things to worry about.

By making happiness the overwhelming dominant positive part of our lives, worrisome things tend to shrink into their proper perspective.

Another way of eliminating much of our worry is to realize there is nothing we can do about things past. And shadows arising on the horizon are often so ill-defined it makes no sense to waste time, energy, and thought on them.

PRAYER: Thank You, God, for Jesus who graphically explains to me that worrying is a useless and needless activity. Help me, O God, to develop a domineering, happy, fun-loving life-style which can overwhelm even those pesky worries of this one day. Amen.

31
Flashing a Prayer

Have you seen a person who was obviously suffering and you wished there was something you could do to help, but couldn't?

Norman Vincent Peale suggested during an interview once that there is something anyone can do regardless of the circumstances. He told this story on himself.

"You remember when railroad trains had club cars on them? Well, I was sitting in a club car once, and a man came in who was terribly drunk," Peale said. "He was offensive, and everybody in the car was annoyed about him and tried to ignore him. Several cussed him out. So, I thought I'd see if a flash prayer would work on this guy. I sat there shooting prayers and imagined him trying to see himself as a better person than he was acting.

"Presently, he gave a big smile and saluted me and said, 'Hi there, Buddy.' And that was all until he got up to stagger out and he came over and shook hands with me. He didn't know me."

Whether a flash prayer has that dramatic an effect or not, it is something anyone can do for anyone else, Peale said. Sometimes people can sense we are concentrating on them and it will have some kind of effect on them as well as on ourselves.

A man who is drunk, causing a disturbance, an angry

woman, a hurt child, someone who is working beside us, or someone we pass in public can all be recipients of our caring, concentrated quickly-aimed prayers.

PRAYER: Dear God, help me to have concern for others, even if all we can do is to mutter a prayer for them in silence. Amen.

32
Working Our Way Through Confusion

Every office has its days when utter confusion seems to reign. Sometimes the confusion can be pinpointed—such as not being able to concentrate because it's Monday morning, or there is a hubbub of talking or shuffling around the office. Sometimes there is confusion from some mysterious source no one can pinpoint.

Confusion around the work place makes it doubly difficult to get the job done. No one can get a mental grasp on set priorities on their work. Even if the confusion can be shoved aside in our minds enough to get things in gear, concentration is difficult, progress is slow, and something isn't right.

A good way to begin is to pick up on some part of your work that requires a minimum of concentration and doesn't take very long. Then stop for coffee or make a trip to the water fountain before tackling the next job. Before long the brain cells will latch onto the fact it must function in spite of the problem and things will soon be on their way.

Paul, in one of his letters to the church at Corinth (1 Cor.14), admonished members to speak one at a time so as not to present a confusion of words. Let two or three prophets speak and then let the others weigh what is said, he said. That way all can learn from each other.

Sometimes there is so much jabbering going on in the office the conflicting sounds melt into gibberish. No wonder we can often get twice as much done in half the time when we take the work home.

I sense that we have become so fascinated with doing things quickly that we sacrifice understanding and overrun our most efficient pace. A noted newspaperman observed that reporters and editors get so mesmerized with the second hand on the clock that sometimes they forget the depth of perception.

Paul said, "God is not a God of confusion, but of peace" (1 Cor. 14:33).

PRAYER: God, I pray to You to help me work through this muddled time. I know that with a little patience, a few gentle nudges, and persistence, my task ahead will become clearer. And I will know that when I finally get a full head of steam, that renewed strength and clear sight will have come from Your hands. Amen.

33
Lonely?

Loneliness or feeling lonely, even in the midst of a crowded office, can be a personally devastating thing. The feelings, the frustrations, and the depression stemming from real or imagined loneliness are very real.

Luckily, there are ways of combating this rather common malady. Even luckier is the fact that most of what can be done does not depend on others. It makes little difference how old you are, although teenagers and older adults seem to feel the frustrations of loneliness the most.

Teenagers, who are awakening to life's possibilities, are still trying to find their way, still trying to gain a sense of belonging. A sense of loneliness is a natural part of the maturing process.

Older adults can feel lonely when the children are grown and have moved out, a mate is lost, friends move away or die, or retirement has separated them from familiar careers.

The in-between ages suffer from loneliness, too, but they are also pulled, tugged, and pushed by children, spouses, bosses, and the myriad of activities connected with those associations. Often, they are too busy to pay attention to passing feelings of loneliness—but when they manage to flop exhausted into a chair the feeling hits them.

Staying busy around a lot of people, however, is not the cure.

One teenage girl who seemed to belong, was the life of every party, and enjoyed the company of the most popular boys. She confessed, however, she was running herself to death trying to keep up with the outwardly happy, laughing, facade of belonging. Inside she was terribly lonely.

Self-analysis is called for. Why do you feel lonely? What attitudes can you change which contribute to a feeling of loneliness? Hyperactive busy-ness, oddly enough, may be a big contributing factor in a feeling of loneliness or separation from others.

Everyone has a basic need for solitude. In solitude we are able to think, to gain inspiration, to put our lives back into proper perspective. In solitude we can be most effective in prayer.

After a particular busy day the apostles came back to Jesus, telling Him all that they had done and taught. "Come away by yourselves to a lonely place, and rest awhile," Jesus told them (Mark 6:31). Jesus did not say to them simply to rest awhile. He said to go to a lonely place to rest. Why?

Because He knew they could not renew themselves mentally and spiritually, as well as physically, unless they could be alone for awhile.

So it is with us. If we stay overly busy day after day, we become weary, wondering if all we do really matters and why all those people out there are not proclaiming our accomplishments.

Loneliness also comes self-made from holding back, from being shy, or from caring more for ourselves than for others. Taking a positive attitude toward a worthwhile project or organization can help you get involved. You'll find people there flocking to you, supporting you, and inviting you into their circle of conversation.

Maybe your feeling of loneliness is because the groups or organizations now taking up your time are no longer suited to your interests. Maybe it is time to decide you can spend your time better somewhere else. Our interests change naturally through life. If we do not change our activities along with that change in interest, we can feel left out, left behind—and lonely.

The psalmist offered a prayer to God: "Turn thou to me, and be gracious to me; for I am lonely and afflicted" (Ps. 25:16).

Sometimes the things we think we are lonely for are not worthy of our time and talents. Life offers almost limitless possibilities. Turning ourselves to other possibilities may be all that is needed to cure a feeling we can do without.

PRAYER: Oh, God, my sense of loneliness is grievous to me. Fill me with initiative that comes from You and is a part of Your vast source of calm confidence. I will spend a few minutes in solitude to give myself time to absorb this power. I will then move out with renewed determination to take my life productive and to take others in. With Your help, my loneliness will fly away and my world will become filled with worthwhile direction and people who need me. Amen.

34
What Others May Think

One of the things which goes with the territory of a job is having to please the boss.

Pleasing the boss can become a worrisome thing if we let it get out of hand. Sometimes we can imagine that every little thing we do or don't do helps or hurts our chances to advance or get fired. Such a mental trap can adversely affect our work.

Beyond the point of being dedicated to your work and doing the best job you can, you don't really have all that much control over what your boss thinks—or anyone else in the office. Allowing yourself to develop a fearful dread over everything you do is emotionally and physically draining.

This has been a problem of my own at times over the years. Now, as a proud, mature citizen, I realize there was absolutely no need to bother. If it is any consolation, those who fear what the boss or the fellow working next to you might be thinking—most people do that. That fear is not confined to those on the low or middle rungs of the ladder of success.

In his biography, Arthur Fiedler, the late famous director of the Boston Pops Orchestra, revealed he had a constant fear of being fired from his job. His fear, of course, was unfounded.

Most of the fears we let become monsters in our minds are blown out of proportion to the truth. Often they are entirely figments of imagination. They probably stem from the fact we tend to be more intolerant with ourselves than is the boss or fellow workers.

This does not mean we should necessarily lower standards for ourselves. It does mean we need to recognize the true situation and not let wild imagination destroy us.

In a letter to Timothy at Ephesus, Paul said to "Take heed to yourself and to your teaching: hold to that, for by so doing you will save both yourself and your hearers" (1 Tim. 4:16). In other words, do good work, but do not be so overly concerned that you neglect your own welfare which might also affect others.

None of us can control the world, or even our own office. We have a difficult enough time trying to control ourselves. Beyond doing our job efficiently as possible, we cannot control very well what anyone else might think.

PRAYER: I am not made to absolutely control others in my life, dear God. So, why is it I feel bothered by the imagined opinions of others when I am doing my job well? Confront me with the choice of doing a job well and being bothered by what others think. Then let me again be filled with Your calming confidence to fulfill my own responsibilities. Amen.

35
Those Who Rule

The Bible speaks often and harshly concerning the responsibilities of those who rule. The biblical writers talk about kings, caesars, and emperors which we translate in our day to dictators, prime ministers, and presidents. But the Bible also speaks of lesser rulers such as princes, governors, and masters which we interpret to mean state governors, mayors, and supervisors.

The point is anyone who is in a position of authority, whether over an entire nation or an office of clerks in a business, carries extra and important responsibilities.

In 2 Samuel is found a section entitled, "Now these are the last words of David" (ch. 23), which deals specifically with those who are in authority.

"The God of Israel has spoken, the Rock of Israel has said to me: When one rules justly over men, ruling in the fear of God, he dawns on them like the morning light, like the sun shining forth upon a cloudless morning, like rain that makes grass to sprout from the earth" (vv. 3-4).

In other words, supervisors are expected to supervise fairly and justly so the people following welcome their leadership. How often, in our human frailties, do we let authority go to our heads once we earn or are given the responsibility?

The great American composer, Randall Thompson, put

those words from 2 Samuel into music, "The Last Words of David," which so beautifully emphasizes their value.

As supervisors, bosses, editors, crew chiefs, project engineers, whatever, we also can emphasis the value of those positions.

PRAYER: Whenever I am in charge and a leader of others, may I realize and accept the tremendous added responsibilities, dear God. May my insight, my motives, my goals be acceptable in Your sight. Help me to apply my leadership with fairness, justice, and a sharing of enthusiasm which those under me will welcome as a morning without clouds. Amen.

36
Kiss Blue Mondays Good-bye

Monday morning blahs! Blah!

We talk about it, complain about it, and then tough it out as if there was nothing we could do to change it. Is there really a way to turn Mondays into productive, enjoyable days? Many have done so.

The first thing to understand is that Monday mornings' flabby unpleasure is probably due to inertia. We've done largely what we wanted to do over the weekend, or not much of anything at all. Then Monday morning comes, and bang, we feel the pressure to perform at top speed and efficiency. We discover the work we must do is far out of reach from the pace we've enjoyed all weekend. The mountain of responsibility sits there staring back.

What to do?

Try something I have pulled on myself. Find the easiest, essential thing you can do first. Concentrate on it and do it without thinking of anything else. Do it as if that were the only thing you had to do all day. Then pick up the next easiest thing and do it the same way, as if when you got it done you could quit and go home.

Next, get that morning cup of coffee, even if it is an hour too early, and greet a co-worker or two. When you get back to your desk, look over all that work and start setting some priorities. Ask yourself what needs to be done first, what needs to be done today, tomorrow, a week from tomorrow.

Suddenly you realize you are launched and the fun is coming back in your job. Why does this work? For me, I think it is because of the organized attack. Picking up something easy to do gives a little jog to the brain cells which isn't too shocking, but still tells those lazy little things to stir a little.

Mondays are essentially "one-thing-at-a-time" days and should be treated as such when we find our minds out of gear. By picking on a few easy tasks at the beginning, we trick our brains into action and they will more readily respond to something easy. Soon, the cells will be talking to each other and say, "Hey, this is fun! Let's keep going!"

It helps to take Monday off the blah list.

PRAYER: My mind is a fascinating thing, dear God. You have given it to me fully equipped to handle about anything I might face—even blah Mondays. May I use this wonderful instrument to keep me forever grateful to

You, realizing that when I allow it to perform I am giving thanks for Your greatness and love. Amen.

37
Wastebasket Theology

Watching a secretary go through a big pile of morning mail, I became more than casually interested when I noticed she was dumping certain envelopes into a nearby large round wastebasket unopened.

She had her orders from the boss, of course, and she was passing by as unimportant the envelopes which had certain identifying words on the outside. This was in spite of the fact that someone had gone to a lot of trouble and expense to create the letters, folders, pamphlets, whatever, which those envelopes contained.

Before condemning such a seemingly flippant view of the day's incoming mail, think of how that matches with what we do to fellow human beings. We meet someone, exchange greetings, maybe even visit a short while, and then dismiss them from our minds without really knowing what they are like on the inside.

It happens all the time, every day.

We have our mind set on the idea that we don't really want another acquaintance like that one. We don't want to overload our social obligations and add someone else to our already long list of people who mean nothing to us.

Others do that to us, of course. The individual we met

last month who never showed much interest in what we were saying, has already written us off as not being worthy of follow-up.

Dealing this way with the morning mail doesn't usually pose much of a problem. In reality, we can often decide quickly if an envelope might contain something we would not be interested in. But with people . . . ?

How many wonderful individuals have we met and discarded because the first quick impression wasn't what we wanted at the moment? Probably more than we would like to admit.

If there is but one thing we ought to remember which Jesus taught, it is that every human being is of limitless worth and is loved by God. Every human being has much to contribute to the world, even though in our feeble way we may not always see what it is.

Whenever we pass off someone as not worth knowing, we are rejecting a part of what God loves, and we are that much poorer ourselves.

PRAYER: I confess, O God, that sometimes I have been in such a dither that I have not taken the time to know a fellow human being new to me. I realize that some of my best friends didn't make too much of an impression on me the first time I met them. Yet, all of them, likable and unlikable, are loved and valued by You. Help me, dear God, to listen and observe and reflect more deeply on my fellow human beings, including the one on the other end of that ringing telephone which is interrupting this prayer. Amen.

38
On Raucous Behavior

It is difficult to put up with the office's overconfident, arrogant, loudmouth. Nothing ever seems to go wrong with him. He plays up to the boss, takes over and dominates office conversations, and seems to be the invincible success story.

Such people manage to make everyone else feel inadequate, patsy, or downright ignorant. It is difficult to realize that these people, too, have their place under the sun in God's scheme of things.

It is also difficult to realize, in the wake of destroyed office harmony, strain on friendships, and raised ire, that the office overachiever may actually be suffering from a hidden major character weakness.

Jesus identified arrogant behavior as hypocritical, someone who is a phony and assumes a fake front. One extensive biblical concordance lists twenty-three times in the New Testament alone where hypocrisy is dealt with.

But, surprise! There are two sides to this problem. As reported in Matthew 7:5 and Luke 6:42, Jesus warns that the log must be removed from the accuser's eye before the speck can be removed from the offender's eye.

Trying to remove the domineering or overbearing character fault from someone else's personality must be preceded by working on our own faults.

Christians, even the rare ones who have few faults, have not been advised by Jesus to cure someone else's faults with a meat-ax. The trick is to make sure the office bully is accepted as a loved human being in spite of obvious weaknesses. He or she may be calling out for help and understanding through displaying objectionable behavior.

PRAYER: Thank You, God, for your Son who has shown me I cannot point to another's faults without having to vividly see my own. Direct my faultfinding ire toward myself first, and then help me to turn my love, concern, and caring attitudes toward others. Amen.

39
The Challenge of Change

J. B. Phillips, in his book *Your God Is Too Small*, makes the point that our own personal worlds may limit our vision of the possible.

If our vision of the outside world is too limited, we are shocked beyond belief even at happenings that normally we should be able to handle.

A supervisor was told by a department head that due to a decrease in business, four employee positions would have to be eliminated. In other words, four people had to be fired. Three of the employees let go, although experiencing the trauma of having to go through the dismissal procedure, took advantage of company help in finding other jobs and began gearing toward a change in careers.

The fourth employee, crushed beyond belief at what was happening, seemed to fall apart emotionally. He chased after everyone in the office he thought could change the decision, pounded on office doors, shouted at his colleagues, and finally, picked up things from his desk and threw them across the room. He calmed down into tearful sobs just as a company guard entered the room.

All four fired employees soon found other jobs. The one who became so emotionally upset found a better job than the other three. In the new job he made more money and had better working hours. In visiting with him later, he admitted the change of jobs was the best thing that could have happened to him.

On a smaller scale such things happen nearly every day in the office. Changes in responsibilities, the installation of computers, changes in the way things are done, changes in supervisors, can be expected at any business which seeks to grow and be successful.

The disciples faced a major change in their lives which none of them handled very well. When Jesus was handed over for trial and ultimate crucifixion, the strain became so great that all of them ran away and hid. Peter even denied he knew Jesus.

But then what happened? After Jesus reappeared to them and they began to accept His new form, they understood more and realized they had become important key elements in the ongoing of Christ's spirit. Their relationships had changed and their jobs had changed. The changes placed much more responsibility on their shoulders—and they accepted. The result was a changed world.

Looking beyond our own small worlds to what might be

possible can be traumatic. Yet, once such a change comes about, we are grateful for the new opportunity. We find expanded responsibilities and a much larger view of the world and its possibilities.

Suddenly being uprooted from our comfortable lives can be a real blessing. Realizing this before we are forced to face dramatic change, makes it easier to accept and take advantage of the doors opening to us.

PRAYER: Dear God, You are much bigger than what I can contain in my own meager brain and spirit. Forgive me when something happens to me and I become upset because my vision of You is too small. I remember that You have given me the power and strength to pick myself up and head for new directions—directions that will take me to bigger and better things in Your name. Amen.

40
Honestly

Being honest means more than not stealing.

Being honest also means carrying out responsibilities honestly.

For instance: People are usually suspicious when a stranger walks up in an overfamiliar way, greets them superwarmly, and pumps their hand over an ear-to-ear grin—action normally reserved for a long-lost brother. Then the stranger starts on his latest sales pitch for insurance.

An employee should also be suspicious when the boss hands out a "promotion" by offering a new title and a different desk without increased responsibilities and pay.

Those who accept at face value such ego-flattering gifts only fool themselves. If they then gloat over others they violate the most sacred standards of honesty.

Jesus used the parable about what happens to seeds which fall on rocks, or in thorns or on good soil. Asked to explain, He said the seed which falls on rocks represent people who hear the word of God, rejoice, but give the word no roots; the seed which falls among thorns represents people who hear the word but are choked by the cares, riches, and pleasures of life.

"And as for that in the good soil, they are those who, hearing the word, hold it fast in an honest and good heart, and bring forth fruit with patience" (Luke 8:15).

PRAYER: Dear God, sometimes I am given gifts which only add another false face to all my other burdensome false faces. Help me to turn these gifts aside with tact and an honest desire not to hurt anyone. With Your help, I can establish and maintain honesty as a testimony to Your greatness. Amen.

41
Seclusion in the Midst of Confusion

In the rush of the day's work with the telephone jangling, co-workers talking and posing questions, the boss asking for some report, and all the other interruptions, haven't you wished you could snap your fingers and be transported into a quiet contemplative corner for a few minutes?

Surprise! It can be done. Many people do it all the time, becoming calm and collected in the midst of the hyperactivity of the workday. I see others do it. I learned to do it myself. How?

First, get acquainted with three very special activities which can calm rattled brains and troubled spirits: Reading, praying, and meditating.

Here is how I have learned to use these three friends:

READING—Carry a small Bible, paperback book of inspiration, or a novel in your purse, attache case, car, or desk. Pull it out to read a page or two whenever there is a break, or at lunch at an isolated table in the company cafeteria, outdoors in a nearby park, or in your car at its parking slot.

MEDITATING—This is more versatile because you can meditate about anything your brain can think up and do it while still at your desk, presumably slaving away at some problem. Better yet, think soaring thoughts (about such things as the Holy Spirit, heaven, etc.) while on your way to the water fountain, while driving your car, while taking in a fresh-air walk around the building, or while walking up and down the stairs trying to get the circulation going again.

PRAYING—Also very versatile, a person can pray almost anywhere at any time. Try a quick, short, one-sentence prayer while hunting for a paper clip or drinking coffee at your desk. Longer prayers are possible, including the Lord's Prayer, while making the trip to the rest room, lunchroom, or walking around inside the office on some duty. What to pray about? Someone else who is ill or facing a difficult situation; yourself over some problem; or a prayer of thanks for the wonderful day you are having.

Any of these three activities can bring a confidence and calmness to a day which otherwise would break you. Doing any of them during the busy day is like leaning back in the chair and slipping into a comfortable old pair of house shoes for a few minutes.

Going to the conference room for a meeting? Get there fifteen minutes early for a few minutes alone. Perfect for prayer or meditation or reading. Traveling by public transportation is great for reading, praying, or meditating. People do it all the time.

Pray between the time it's lights out at bedtime and the time when you drift into sleep. Or, if you wake up in the middle of the night and can't go back to sleep, use that time to meditate or pray. Turning on the light and reading for thirty minutes or an hour can calm the sleepless brain.

This program is highly flexible and can be fitted into anyone's work schedule. It is a matter of finding those little bits of time and using them to the best advantage.

PRAYER: Dear God, I bring myself to the realization I don't have to be busy every minute of every day while I work. Thank You for pointing out those patches of time you have provided for me as hidden refuges for mental and spiritual renewal. I will use them as gifts from You. Amen.

42
Must We Judge Others?

Someone posed the question: "How can we judge the deeds of others when so much of the time we can't understand what we do ourselves?"

The question opens our thoughts on what is judgment? How can we make choices or decisions, especially when it involves things other people do, without making us feel we are trying to take God's place?

Jesus said, "Judge not, that you be not judged" (Matt. 7:1).

Does this mean that whenever someone cuts in front of us in the cafeteria line and we have mean thoughts about that person, we are doing something Jesus told us not to do? Does judgment include passing views and opinions which might temporarily fill our minds and then disappear?

The dictionary definition of judgment tends to lean toward a serious connotation. Judgment is the weighing of evidence and pronouncing a decision more or less as a final irrevocable action, most dictionaries say.

Our own personal passing wisp of an opinion of someone's action does not seem to be included in the act of judgment. Our decision in favor of or against the actions of a co-worker do not seem to become judgments unless we set that decision in concrete or take action based on that decision.

Let us follow Jesus' reasoning further. Jesus said if we are going to judge someone, we must remember that we, ourselves, are also subject to judgment and all the personal damage that may mean.

An opinion we may make about someone in our own minds, and then forget, would not be judgment within the context Jesus talked about.

An opinion announced in public so as to condemn someone does not become a judgment if we subsequently retract our judging action and offer apologies.

The forgiveness on the part of others who suffer from our rash decision against them, also releases us from a charge of being judgmental.

Refusing to associate with someone because they once did something we didn't like, is judgment. Reaccepting that person as a friend, cancels out that judgment and does what Jesus has admonished us to do.

Paul, or someone writing in Paul's name, advised members of the church at Colossae that if a member has a complaint against another, forgive each other as the Lord has forgiven.

The point is, we can't avoid making personal choices

and decisions. It is when we make such decisions and let them stand as permanent condemnations of others that the decisions become judgments which are condemned by God.

PRAYER: Let not our passing thoughts about others become permanent judgments, Dear God, but thoughts which are immediately followed by a forgiving, caring, reconciliating attitude. Amen.

43
The Irritant

Every office has one, it seems—the person who irritates everyone else and makes teamwork almost impossible, or at least most difficult.

Don't you know people who must always be right, always know the latest office secret before anyone else, need to be loved by everyone constantly, must go out and buy the latest thingamajig everyone else is buying, are always the first to organize a party for the office newlyweds, blame problems and mistakes on everyone else, try to dominate, and talk constantly?

Such people do not realize they are irritating those around them and do not seem to realize they have lost friends and potential friends.

A man who fits into this category where I once worked has the habit of bragging almost constantly of how he takes revenge against the car mechanic, the telephone company, the paperboy, even his wife, when he senses wrongdoing on the part of others. He is a constant talker and goes into great detail to justify his hatred and actions of revenge.

When he comes to the coffee break, most soon find an excuse to get back to their desks.

There is a lesson in this for each of us. To a certain degree, more or less, we all have habits and say things that irritate others. Listening to others who overdo their irritations so grandly, can tune us into listening and being conscious of ourselves.

In group conversations, people do not relish anyone who dominates the conversation for very long. Certainly they are not interested in gripes, personal hates, and actions of revenge, or the latest incident when someone else has done them in.

People listen intently, however, when someone is praised, or an interesting and unusual experience is told for the first time, or some personal positive victory is related which stirs feelings of empathy.

Those kinds of conversations are relaxing and make people feel good about going back to work after the midmorning or midafternoon coffee break.

PRAYER: Dear God, let me remember first that I should forever be in a forgiving mood toward those who are irritating. Let me remember that I also have irritating habits which need working on. Let me begin today by finding an irritating habit of my own for You to change or eliminate. Amen.

44
Empathetically

It takes difficult conscious effort to attain empathy with others—the ability to develop a sympathetic awareness of another's presence and feelings.

Sometimes it takes training. In others it seems to come naturally. However empathetic ability is developed and attained, we need it in order to understand what is happening in our private worlds and why people do and say the things they do and say.

At a restaurant with a friend, we were fortunate to be waited upon by an attractive young woman who had an outgoing, bubbly personality. On our way to the cash register I made a point of telling her how much we appreciated her service and attitude. Her eyes lit up even more. She put her hand on my shoulder and wished us a great day.

I wouldn't trade anything for those little experiences during my work week. They are usually brief and come unexpectedly, but are like jewels, helping to set a joyful tone for the rest of the day.

They are the small gifts of God's world which come as extras in our lives, making our existence sparkle.

PRAYER: Thank You, God, for the unexpected little diamonds of our day. We can't buy them, we can't even expect them, but they come like bits of flashing joy, re minding us again that life is worth living and living abundantly. May we, in turn, be empathetic bits of joy to others. Amen.

45
Laughing Through the Day

A fellow worker, whenever she cannot find a report atop her paper-littered desk, announces, "I can't find a piece of paper." The habitual saying has become an office joke. A co-worker decided he would play a trick the next time she said that.

Only a few days later the woman again announced, "I can't find a piece of paper." The man opened his desk drawer and said, "Here it is," waving above his head for all to see, a single square of toilet tissue.

Everyone laughed, including the victim, fortunately.

Humor is a welcomed element in any office. It breaks up the overly serious aspects of our jobs. Humor, of course, can be overdone and can become obnoxious, pointedly sarcastic, or an avenue of ridicule. But sincere and spontaneous laughter during the working day makes life more fun. It is a gift of God to be able to laugh in the midst of carrying out our responsibilities, even if at ourselves.

Although Christianity is usually treated as a serious subject and the Bible a serious book, there are lighter moments and humor.

Much biblical humor is based on wordplay and puns

and much is lost in translation from the original Greek or Hebrew. Yet, the humor still often shines through.

Abraham and Sarah, living in the twilight of their years, thought it extremely funny when they understood God's message that they were to produce an offspring.

"Then Abraham fell on his face and laughed" at the prospect God was going to cause a son to be delivered to them (Gen. 17:17).

"And Sarah said, 'God has made laughter for me; every one who hears will laugh over me' " (Gen. 21:6).

There are other examples in the Old Testament endorsing laughter:

"Strength and dignity are her clothing, and she laughs at the time to come" (Prov. 31:25).

"A time to weep, and a time to laugh" (Eccl. 3:4).

"He will yet fill your mouth with laughter" (Job 8:21).

"Then our mouth was filled with laughter" (Ps. 126:2).

Jesus held laughter in high regard:

"Blessed are you that weep now, for you shall laugh" (Luke 6:21).

"Why do you see the speck that is in your brother's eye, but do not notice the log that is in your own eye?" (Matt. 7:3).

"You blind guides, straining out a gnat and swallowing a camel!" (Matt. 23:24).

Even the serious and gruff Paul enjoyed relating a situation which probably evoked laughter: "To the unmarried and the widows I say that it is well for them to remain single as I do. But if they cannot exercise self-control, they should marry. For it is better to marry than to be aflame with passion" (1 Cor. 7:8-9).

PRAYER: Thank You, God, that laughter is a great gift as a part of the life you have given us. May we enjoy it in healthy hilarity and share it with others. Amen.

46
Failed Projects

After temporarily putting aside other responsibilities and investing effort, time, and company expense to complete a special project, an employee was told the project would be dropped.

Although there are overriding company responsibilities involving such situations, this kind of situation can be devastating for self-esteem, for employee relations, and to the enthusiasm which was generated for the special project.

Unless told otherwise, the employee must assume the special project job was done well. To unfairly accept blame for a project gone wrong or suddenly dropped ignores a hundred other reasons plans can be changed.

This is where the value of hope comes to our rescue. A new project, other responsibilities, and thousands of future opportunities offer the hope and probability that the next project will be productive and successful.

The classic demonstrations of this are the failures and successes of Jesus and His disciples. Jesus' hometown ignored, even ridiculed Him. Some of the disciples broke away or failed their responsibilities at inopportune times.

Yet, overall, what an impact their lives had on the world. Great authors, composers, architects, teachers—all know the pangs of real or imagined failure. They also know of joyous success and victory.

Those of us who help make up the vast numbers of humanity, and who also have influence on some of them, are no different.

PRAYER: We have the power to learn from and then discard the great failures in our lives, dear God. This power allows us to move on with enthusiastic determination toward doing it right the next time. Thank You, God, for the bounce-back power You have given us. Amen.

47
On a Positive Note

A good-looking young man in our office was recently promoted to a higher position of responsibility. He well deserved it.

He is a thoughtful, energetic fellow who makes those under him feel they are working with him, rather than for him. He makes everyone working around him feel important and that what they do is important. Everyone working with him feels they are a part of the team. He is one of the rare sources of positive anticipation in the office.

It is a joy to watch him operate.

You probably have known people like that where you work or have worked in the past. They are not to be feared. They are to be encouraged. Tell them about your thumbs-up feeling for them.

PRAYER: Thank You, dear God, for empathetic leaders who attain their station in life through work and thoughtful intelligence and who leave a trail of sincere lasting friendships in their wake. Amen.

48
Goodness On a Shaggy Day

Dull days bore a lot of people. A better term for dull days or days lacking in excitement and activity is—neutral days.

Thank God for neutral days. Otherwise we would have nothing as a standard to compare days of high excitement or tragic consequences. A day when there are no major problems, no sudden rush jobs, no unwanted surprises, when everything goes reasonably well, ought to be as welcome as the ice-cream wagon on a hot summer day.

On days when people don't bother you with useless frivolity and dumb questions and you can go home at the end of the office day satisfied you've completed a good work load, is a time for gratefulness, even celebration.

PRAYER: So few of our days are neutral, dear God. We can be thankful that we are blessed with them, usually in the nick of time, when we can be comfortable in our work, enjoy our friends and go home contented. Thank You, God, for neutral days. Amen.

49
The Office Talker

Among the things which boldly grab time in the office is the talker. Ecclesiastes is blunt about this.

"A time to keep silence, and a time to speak" (Eccl. 3:7).

A young man, highly talented, dependable, and hardworking, has one very irritating habit. He talks every subject to death. Ask him a question or casually bring up a subject, and he takes over. His brain goes numb and he locks his mouth and voice in gear telling everything he knows, every experience he has had, and every opinion he has developed on the subject, related and unrelated. His ears turn off to everything anyone else says. It soon becomes obvious he is interested only in hearing himself talk.

There is no dialogue or genuine conversation with others. The only way to get out of the sticky situation is to walk off or blow up.

One day, another worker who got caught listening to the man's long-winded tirade, finally interrupted in a loud voice.

"You don't understand my problem, motor-mouth. Bug off!" Motor-mouth turned on his heels and stalked off, muttering obscenities. Others in the office smiled or snickered, probably wondering why they hadn't had the nerve to fight back.

An hour later he had another victim helplessly wondering how to get out of the same trap.

Each of us have been guilty, too. We cheapen our words by using a thousand when ten would do. We produce more words than our listeners want to hear. We make beautiful language terribly inefficient.

Recognizing the problem in ourselves is most of the battle. Each of us have deceived ourselves into thinking that what we have to say is more important than what anyone else has to say. We love to hear our own voices broadcast those giant gems of self-obtained wisdoms.

One of the most important things writers and speakers must learn is how to express ideas and information in as few words as possible. It is a difficult and tedious learning process. Teachers, editors, and others who ride herd on writers, must be relentless in reducing the use of words to the minimum. This applies to news stories in print or on television and radio, as well as blockbusting fiction for books and drama on stage, screen, or video.

Printing, paper, and electronic airtime is costly. The personal time of readers and listeners is valuable. Making our words more efficient is one of the challenges of life which is worth the effort.

It can make the difference between rejection as a motor-mouth and acceptance as someone having valuable things to say. Those looked up to as interesting and authoritative do not necessarily have more important things to say. But they express themselves in fewer words which are precise and carry impact.

PRAYER: Thank You, God, for Jesus who had so much to say and so little time in which to say it. Jesus' entire dialogue would not fill the pages of a modern novel. But look at the impact. As He is our example, help us to stop trashing words and learn how to express ourselves more efficiently. In Your name, Amen.

50
Lemon Days

After driving to work on a dreary and rainy morning, I got into the elevator with a friend.

"I could go back home and curl up with a good book," she said with a sigh.

Such thoughts are said as much to ourselves as to others. We would just as soon not be at work on certain days, thinking of a hundred other things we would rather be doing—or doing nothing.

And that's OK, really.

When those kinds of moods come over us, we are actually working at getting our priorities in order. We may be thinking of major life-changing ideas. *Is this job really worth it? Do I need the money? Would I be happier in some other occupation? Is this the time to strike out on my own?*

Or, minor things. *What can I do to reorganize my work day and make it easier and more interesting? How can I get more done in the time I have? How can I reserve more time at home to curl up with a good book?*

Picking up on a particular mood, propping it up, and looking at it in the face can spark a creative chain of thoughts. This we need for self-examination leading to corrections in our personal life-style and attitudes.

Squeezing lemon days to make lemonade thoughts can turn a dampening mood into hope and joyous expectation.

PRAYER: Thank You, dear God, for this wonderful mind and spirit which can generate within itself a rekindling of hope, change, and enthusiasm. We may not be able to change the world, or even our personal circumstances on our own, but with the power You have given us we can change our outlook and find ways to make other changes which may surprise us. Amen.

51
Dishing Out Criticism

As an attack weapon, criticism can be a powerfully destructive force. When used with a sense of justice and empathy, constructive criticism can be a positive stimulation.

Criticism today seems to carry a negative connotation that is unfair to the word.

The apostle Paul criticized the early church, but the way he did it was a valuable lesson for us. Paul did not dwell on the demeaning implications of the church's problems.

In his first letter to the church at Corinth, only about a dozen of the 436 verses directly criticize the Corinthian Christians. The rest of the letter contains praise, instruction, or answers to questions.

Paul uses several instructional methods to avoid direct destructive criticism. We can use these tactics as well, and should, when we find ourselves in the uncomfortable position that criticism seems the most direct and effective route.

Paul used questions most effectively. When members of the church seemed to be using worldly wisdom as their guideline, Paul asked, "Has not God made foolish the wisdom of the world?" (1 Cor. 1:20).

Paul also appealed to the Corinthians' faith and the direction of their growth in the church—"For consider your call, brethren" (1 Cor. 1:26).

Placing himself in the context as a brother, Paul appealed to their high sense of responsibility. "This is how one should regard us, as servants of Christ and stewards of the mysteries of God" (1 Cor. 4:1).

Paul answered their questions. "Now concerning the matters about which you wrote . . . " (1 Cor. 7:1).

Paul wished the best for each man, appealing to each man's desire for positive living. "I want you to be free from anxieties" (1 Cor. 7:32).

Paul also commended the Corinthians in everything he saw they were doing right. He did this many times throughout his letters, keeping in context the criticisms he makes and the instructions he sends in friendship. He opens and closes his letters with praise and thanksgiving.

Thus, Paul is a valuable base on which we can handle justifiable and positive criticism of others.

PRAYER: God, help us to realize criticism should be used sparingly and only when it can be a positive force of support. Sheath our criticism as a weapon and make it constructive, instructive, and questioning. In Your name, Amen.

52
Do You Feel Guilty When You're Caught Up?

People who like their job and are dedicated to their work feel guilty whenever a day comes along when there isn't much to do. They make-do work and try to look busy, all the while seething with tension inside. They wish fervently they had something worthwhile to do.

In our hyperactive society, we feel useless and out of place whenever our jobs require just being there and available. To many people, if they are not overloaded, slaving until their bones ache, and putting in extra hours, they aren't working.

Burnout and hypertension are real problems. They affect the quality of work and rob people of efficiency and job enjoyment.

Overload is not unavoidable sometimes. Every office occasionally goes through the need to hump it and do extra duty. But as a constant normal situation, overload is a bummer.

A light work-load day is a blessing in disguise. Such a

day allows each person to put job responsibilities into perspective, provides time to contemplate how to be more efficient, and allows a chance to clean off the desk and start that new file system.

PRAYER: God, why do I feel so guilty when I have nothing to do for the moment and I look up to see if the boss is watching? I'm doing my job well, I can remember those days when I worked late or took a satchel of work home, or put in hard days without breaks or lunch. Help me keep all this in perspective. Amen.

53
Hooray for the Office Break!

What do you do on your mid-morning or mid-afternoon break? You goof off, of course. It seems to be a stupid question.

It may surprise you that office breaks are often misused and don't really bring back resilience and eager work attitudes.

The reason for office breaks is to break up the routine and to refresh ourselves so we can go back to work with renewed vigor, energy, and interest.

Too often, however, we simply continue talking shop or do things which are not much different than the work. Two minutes after going back to the job, we feel just as tired and done in as we did before the break. We might as well have ignored the break.

What are some creative ways of using breaks so we feel good about going back to work?

First, let's do a little putting-all-this-into-perspective thinking.

It is surprising how long a ten- or fifteen-minute break can seem and what can be accomplished. What needs to be accomplished depends on what your work is like.

A work schedule requiring standing and operating a machine certainly calls for sitting down, even lying down, and going through a relaxing routine. (See the chapter titled "Tension.") Someone who is sitting down most of the time needs to get up and walk vigorously, even if doing nothing more than walking around the building or up and down an inside stairway.

Someone who gets up and down constantly and seldom sees another person during work, may need a quiet conversation with someone in a corner of the break room with a cup of hot coffee in hand.

Here are some specific activities which you are invited to shop through and which fit your needs best:

—For those who have sedentary or inert jobs: Walk around the block. Explore some area of the business or building where you work that you've never seen before. Go get a cold or hot drink with a friend or read the bulletin board while drinking. Stand up, stretch, make a call to spouse or friend while standing. If there are stores nearby, go shopping for some little tidbit you need at home, like dental floss, a comb, a birthday card, or shampoo.

—For those with jobs requiring constant standing or physically active responsibilities: Read a book or magazine. Rest in the company cafeteria or refreshment room or nearby cafe over a cold or hot drink with a friend. Keep

stationery and stamps handy; find an empty desk and
write a short note to a friend or the children. Call up your
spouse or a friend on the telephone for a short visit while
sitting down. Find a spot to sit and think awhile, or lay
down on the carpeted floor.

—For longer breaks such as lunch periods or activities
for jobs of a general nature: Go to the nearest library and
check out a book. Gather a few others, go to a conference
room or unused office, close the door, and sing songs. Find
a place to lie down or slouch in a chair with feet propped
up, close eyes, and meditate. Bring pad and pencil and
work on that great American novel. Wash your face with
a damp paper towel. Massage face gently with fingers to
loosen muscles. Rub hands with hand lotion to make
them feel good. Exercise, giving neck, arms, legs, torso a
short workout. Go to a private place, take a seat, close
eyes, and clear all thoughts out of head, thinking of a
pleasant scene or a prayer.

PRAYER: A creative mind is our greatest asset, dear
God. Help us use our minds to greatest advantage, active
or restful, whenever we are given gifts of time. The gift of
time is one of the most valuable we can receive. Help us
use it wonderfully. Amen.

54
Enjoy the Smoothies

I'm not talking here about the sophisticated boys from the big city. The smoothies are those days when everyone seems to be deep in their work, there are few interruptions, and the work flow is going along nicely, thank you.

Perhaps all the bosses are in the office at the same time, or maybe none of them are. Maybe there has been a change in the weather, or tomorrow is a holiday and so much work must be completed. Whatever the reason, a quiet busy office is a rarity when it ought to be the norm.

Take advantage of it and enjoy the near-perfect working conditions.

It is my contention that many offices are not very well designed. Most office systems defy efficiency and the normal working conditions are constant interruptions. Most offices offer poor working conditions.

So, when everything is going smoothly, the only noise is the hum of a few office machines and everyone is short on speech and long on courtesy, work away and enjoy.

PRAYER: Dear God, we have so few perfect setups in our lives. Help us to enjoy them while they are available. We give thanks for such days among the many which are hubbub, confusing, and hyperactive. Thank you for calm strength. Amen.

55
When You Want to Apologize

You can't stand Joe. You got in an argument one day over how he ought to be doing his job and he told you to buzz-off. You walk away in a huff and have hardly said a word to him since.

Now, you realize what you did was childish and it really wasn't your place to criticize his work. In fact, actually, you see now he is quite efficient. Everyone else likes Joe. You want to like him, too. But you don't feel you can just walk up and apologize. That would be embarrassing. So, what can you do?

Adjust your own feelings and attitudes so you can go to Joe and face up to the situation with the confidence you are doing the right thing in the right way at the right time. And you want to show Joe your own confidence that he is the likable chap he seems to be, that you want to brush off the whole incident and carry on as a friend.

Jesus had a lot to say about how to reconcile yourself with another person.

"So if you are offering your gift at the altar, and there remember that your brother has something against you, leave your gift there before the altar and go; first be reconciled to your brother, and then come and offer your gift" (Matt. 5:23-24).

Before you can consider yourself complete and righteous, you must make up with your brother (or sister), Jesus is saying. That is the first order of business.

In most offices, chance encounters place everyone in contact with everyone else at one time or another. Jesus is saying, however, that special effort should be made to meet the adversary as early as possible. If a chance encounter does not bring you and the other fellow to the water fountain or lunch counter soon, then make a point to have coffee together or simply walk over to the other person's desk.

Be sincerely friendly. Show interest in his or her work or hobbies or family. Continue this interest following the apology. This helps to cement good relationships and builds a base upon which a solid friendship can develop.

PRAYER: Dear God, help me to realize again that every person is precious and valuable to You. When there is disagreement, help me avoid lasting anger and to develop a willingness to patch things up when my anger gets out of control. I look to You for the strength of peace as I rectify my separation from others. Amen.

56
So You've Had a Rough Day Today?

All work days are different—some better than others, of course. On this particular day, nothing goes right. You complain—about the working conditions, about those around you, about the company—subconsciously trying to gain sympathy on your plight. What you get is a call from the boss to come to his office.

The boss chews you out. You go back to your desk feeling terrible and subdued. You don't want to talk to anyone. You realize if you had felt that way earlier you wouldn't be in trouble with the boss now.

How do you handle such a situation from a Christian and a practical viewpoint?

From experience you know the bad work day is not normal. Bad-mouthing about it, which ticked off the boss, is also not normal and will probably pass.

What Jesus said about loving our enemies can also apply to such enemies as frustration, hopelessness, disappointment, and depression. Does this mean we must love frustration, hopelessness, disappointment, and depression?

Look at it this way. To paraphrase an old saying,"Adversity is the mother of invention." The adversities of frustration, hopelessness, disappointment, and depression have been used by many as launching pads for ideas and enthusiasm which overcome those problems.

Haven't you known people who faced problems which spurred them on to try other ways of solving those problems? Jesus did. He faced all of them and showed us how to conquer them.

Self-assessment is the first order of business. It must be determined exactly what is the problem. Second is exploring ways of going around, under, over, or through the situation.

With a bad workday, talking over your frustrations

with a trusted friend or companion helps to keep the situation under control. If that is impossible, a short prayer at your desk, in the coffee room, in the rest room, or over lunch is a big help. Walking around the building, breathing deeply the fresh outside air, does wonders for brain cells.

PRAYER: You have endowed me with feelings, dear God, which occasionally I let get out of control. But You have also given me the strength to overcome those feelings. Help me to recognize, before it is too late, when a situation is getting out of control. I draw on the strength which comes only from Your hands to meet my needs of the day and the hour. Amen.

57
But We've Never Done It That Way Before

All of us in our varied tasks learned how to do it best, either by experience or through instruction, and then set it in our minds. We lock out subsequent changes as not worthy of consideration.

Jesus ran across this continually during His ministry. He stirred up so much animosity that certain groups decided He would have to be put to death to keep the public order.

Healing on the sabbath created one such problem. The

people accusing Jesus of breaking the sabbath law ignored what was important.

People then, as well as ourselves today, seek excuses for doing things the same old way rather than thinking over the matter. Instead of trying to understand a better way which fits the spirit of the activity, we use vast amounts of effort to justify why things should be done as they have always been done.

Mankind never improved his lot, nor managed to understand better what God is saying through the Scriptures, by doing everything the same way it had been done since the beginning of time.

PRAYER: Dear God, You expect me to use my physical body, my mind, my spirit with care, innovation and eagerness—qualities which come from You. Help me to avoid moribund roteness, a sort of living death into which we humans occasionally fall. Our joy is in living the life You have given us. Amen.

58
So, You've Been Fired!

Being fired from the job is the ultimate in bad office experiences. Or, so we think. Most people feel being fired is the near-death experience from the office family with which you've become familiarly comfortable. Yet, much of what happens after you have been separated from your job and income depends directly on yourself.

First, let us put the padding of perspective around the experience of being fired. Getting fired is not all that unusual. Lots of people get fired. Every day. Getting fired may put you into a rather exclusive group, depending on how well you are able to make hay out of the happening.

A lot of highly successful, famous people have been fired at some time during their careers. They were able to turn the experience around and managed to become better off than before they were fired. Sometimes in surprisingly short order.

Getting fired is not necessarily a reflection on your own abilities, dedication, loyalty or willingness to work hard at your assigned tasks. The company may be having financial troubles and in order to stay afloat, the boss must let people go. The boss might have had a bad week and the president of the firm laid the law down to him that morning.

Then again, maybe you haven't been doing too good a job. You can change that and can do better next time. For there will be a next time, and a next, and a next.

Depending on your own personality, the first few minutes after being fired brings on different reactions.

One young man I know was fired and experienced rather vividly all the symptoms of grief. First, there was the initial shock of what was happening, then disbelief and denial it was happening, then anger, and finally an attempt to bargain away the firing experience followed by depression and eventual acceptance.

This young man could have moved in any of three directions: Growth, chronic stress, or disaster leading to mental illness and alienation. He took growth, sought another job and has since successfully filled a much more satisfying position. Also with better pay, I might add.

Others take a more flippant attitude about getting fired and come out on top faster and seemingly without visible stress or strain. They may have hidden strong emotional feelings underneath their frivolity. But they often land other successful jobs as quickly or quicker than those who go through the grieving process.

A good example of this is a friend who was asked by his boss to step into his office as soon as a telephone call could be completed. The friend had to wait fifteen minutes. In the meantime quitting time came and went.

When he entered the office the boss told him he had been fired. My friend quickly retorted, "You can't fire me on my personal time. My workday ended ten minutes ago. Wait until tomorrow."

The end result was, my friend told me, that he got another day's pay out of the company and had time to start making plans for another job before the expected firing took place the next morning.

Another friend, who was fired on a Friday, told me the following Monday that she already had two new jobs to choose from. Her problem was deciding which one to take. Both of them were in her field of expertise and both paid more than she had been earning.

Accepting a job at less pay than before is no insult. The new job may provide faster promotion. And, there is no law that says you must keep that job forever if something better comes along.

If firing comes because of poor performance on the job, or you even suspect that might be at least partially the reason, you'll need to sit down in some quiet, undisturbed space and do some thinking. Maybe you didn't like the job to begin with, or there was a clash of personalities. Whatever the reason, it is up to you to recognize it and seek employment where those factors are absent or will not become a factor.

Maybe further training or education is the answer. Maybe your own mental attitudes need changing. Maybe moving to another geographical location—another city or state—would help. Adjusting attitudes, abilities, or location are good preventive measures in order to make the next job a success.

Even if the firing was over something you could not control, improved attitudes and abilities can only improve your situation, your happiness, and your effectiveness.

Poor old Job, as related in the biblical story, lost everything he had, including much of his family and even his health. But he hung in there with his faith in God and eventually was restored.

The story of Job graphically demonstrates what can and often does happen by not caving in to setbacks, disappointments, and major tragedies.

Paul, in his letter to the Ephesians, said, "Pray at all times in the spirit, with all prayer and supplication. To that end keep alert with all perseverance" (Eph. 6:18).

Everyone realizes the comfort of close friends and relatives. In addition, the Christian realizes the comfort of prayer, of God, and of fellow Christians.

The crisis of being fired doesn't need to be a crisis.

After the shock of being fired, prayer, a period of self-examination—get to work. If your immediate need is another pay check and jobs are hard to find, take advantage of every idea and source of help you can locate.

Many companies offer help in relocating in another job, even if the firing was done in anger. Get out the old resume, update it and send it out or take it to prospective employers. Work with government and private employment agencies, buttonhole friends for contacts, fill out every employment application form for every kind of job you think you would like to tackle. Don't let any moss grow under those shoes.

And keep praying.

PRAYER: Oh, God, in my hour of anguish, I know You are with me as always. All I need to do is to accept the calming strength that comes from Your hands, and this I do right now, at this very moment. Shrink my fears, dear God, and take from my shoulders the heavy difficulties I feel. Turn my heart and head from vengeance, put my problems and my fears behind me and let me look to the future with hope and with confidence. I draw on Your strength and tap my innermost abilities for I am going to come out on top. So help me, in Jesus' name. Amen.

59
Living Lighter

I know you've seen them in your office. They walk in at the beginning of the workday with a face set in stone. When you greet them with a cheery, "Hello," they mutter something between a grunt and a burp, if they respond at all.

It's more fun to live the lighthearted life.

One day I saw a veteran of the office greet a young employee with, "Hello, Miss Young." She responded with, "Hello, Mr. Old." Her name wasn't Young and his name wasn't Old. Both smiled and went on their way, knowing they had lightened the workday a bit for each other.

Have you noticed that people who joke friendly seem to enjoy life more? Whether people joke to sweep away the gloomies, or joke because they are high on life at the moment, makes little difference. The effect is still good.

Happiness can stem from a bursting from within the heart, a celebration that it is good to be alive and kicking. Happiness can also spring from just acting happy and cutting down the size of whatever may be bothersome.

Humming a pleasant tune when a problem hits the desk helps ease the brain into solving gear. It is surprising how hope for the day can be revitalized simply by choosing it.

PRAYER: God, thank You for this day of new opportunity and the chance to prove to myself again that my every need is available from Your hands. May I find Your rejuvenating strength welling up inside and bursting through my mind and spirit. Amen.

60
Make It Funny

A sense of humor is a God-given gift we all have. The ones who let humor have its way during part of the workday have discovered an outlet for boundless joy as well as a way to bolster sagging spirits.

An ability to detect the funnies in whatever it is we do for a living indicates good emotional health. The one who finds something to smile, giggle, or laugh at once in awhile is also the source of mental health for fellow workers.

Sometimes an entire business can manage to laugh at itself in public. Note this classified advertisement which appeared recently in a large daily newspaper:

> We are interested in hiring 7 semi-obnoxious, pushy sales pros, for a very boring repetitious job of selling. Our rather dismal office is located at . . . and you'd be forced to work in the office. Our current staff, which is the laziest group of individuals you will ever see, drag themselves to work, Mon-Sat to decide whether to complain about the weather, the coffee, the thermostat or the manager. When that's all over, they somehow manage to organize themselves, work their appointments and sell a whole lot. Which is surprising, because nobody wants to buy anything we sell, because our prices are too high and the economy stinks. Applicants should have a skin like an alligator and desire to suffer their way to a $25,000+ per

year job. If interested contact . . .

Humor helps smooth the day, especially when we learn how to laugh at ourselves.

In the office where I work, the chirping telephone is the most irritating interruption. Yet, the telephone is essential, in spite of the large numbers of crank calls, wrong numbers, and hang ups.

Some who find themselves holding an empty line in their ear quickly hang up and say loudly so everyone can hear, "You're another!" This faked response invariably brings smiles or a laugh.

Computer terminals adorn every desk in our office. They are the saviors as well as the banes of newswriting. They also play a part in office humor.

One likable reporter came to work one morning to find the words, "Dear Ann," followed by an entire screen filled with "Good Morning, Good Morning, Good Morning, etc.. . . ." At the bottom of the screen were the words, "Erasing this message will cause dire consequences."

After she smiled and looked around wondering who did the "cute" deed, she punched the keys clearing the screen. At that same moment, one of her fellow workers popped an air-filled paper bag, sending a muscle-jerking explosion through the newsroom. Ann burst out laughing. Her day had been launched in style.

Needless to say, that kind of trick would not be appreciated at deadline time during the work day. Humor can get out of hand for those who do not recognize what is in good taste and permissible and what is simply disruptive.

Any office completely devoid of humor is probably an inefficient operation with high tension and job insecurity.

Humor makes the difference between a satisfying career and a drag.

PRAYER: Thank You, God, for the funny bones you have installed in each of us. May we use that feature of our character with trust, intelligence, and wholesome fun which neither ridicules others nor needlessly disrupts the services customers expect from us. Amen.

61
Recharging Ourselves

Jesus demonstrated His thorough understanding of human need when He withdrew from the crowds to go someplace alone to pray.

What we may self-diagnose as depression or lackluster performance at the office may simply be an overload on the brain and spirit. At regular times we need to let our thinking and meditating capacity catch up to reality.

This probably cannot be done effectively during the office day, but needs the uncluttered and open-ended time of an entire evening or an entire day or weekend.

The person who works hard all week and then dives into busy activities through every evening and the weekend, is not allowing time for needed rejuvenation and communion with God. That person is not ready to go back to work on Monday morning.

My wife, Helen, and I have learned over the years that we need to withdraw several times during the month. In order to do that we schedule relaxing times as if they were vitally important activities. And they are. We think such withdrawals are important enough to turn down invitations from friends, to avoid trips to the store, and to ignore the telephone—at least for a few hours or an evening.

Sometimes, if the day or week has been particularly frantic, the withdrawal will involve minimum activity as a bridge between our busy schedules and the complete inactivity. So we watch television, or go to a play or concert or movie, or roam around a shopping mall—then get plenty of sleep. The first chance we get after that, we schedule the inactivity.

The inactivity bars answering telephone and doorbell, sitting quietly to read or think up beautiful thoughts and prayers. Calm, low-key conversation is sometimes relaxing in this context.

In addition to this, we have regular prayer and devotional time just before bedtime. If we can manage to get to bed early enough we may read until sleep comes.

The human condition must be allowed to recharge itself. If we do not recharge, we risk a hyperactive life that threatens our health, or opens the door to mental illness and creates a life that is busy on the surface but has little depth of meaning.

PRAYER: Dear God, as I pause to recharge myself with the calm, confident strength which comes from You, slow my hectic pace to the comfort zone of my body. Let me gather the quiet reserves needed to face my daily responsibilities with assurance and determination. Amen.

62
Thinking Away the Bad

A song by Paul Sjolund contains these words:
"Out of my sorrow I shall make a song so beautiful that others' grief will cease."

There is a certain amount of truth to the idea that to be happy, a person merely needs to act happy.

Abraham Lincoln is quoted as having said, "Most folks are as happy as they make up their minds to be." This is to say that each of us can do much to control the moods and anxieties which flow over us each day.

Nearly anyone can stand most situations for one working day. All God expects us to do is to live one day at a time.

Sorrow, grief, disappointment, harassment, boredom, anxiety, and anger may come to us unexpected and unwelcomed. But each of us has the God-given capacity to overcome these feelings, if not actually do away with them.

Tapping into our internal spiritual strength can counteract the emotional upheavals which the workaday world throws at us.

How is this practical? What must we do to tap into this spiritual strength?

A man I know has a down-to-earth way of doing this. When faced with a particularly difficult period, he takes time out to go get an ice-cream cone, a candy bar, or goes over to a co-worker and tells that person what a good job they are doing. He might simply tell someone a joke, or smile to himself and hum a tune as if he didn't have a care in the world.

He told me that such an action draws strength from within that usually reduces the magnitude of the problem and brings it within a manageable perspective.

If he is faced with a drastic downhill slide of his emotions, he turns to prayer. He said he usually gets up from his desk and walks down the hall, concentrating on a short prayer.

PRAYER: Lord, just for today, I will adjust myself to whatever is, and not try to change the world to my own desires. Just for today, I will look for some beauty in everything and enjoy it. Amen.

63
Peace of Mind

Duke University did a study comparing people who had peace of mind with those who were unhappy and under pressure. The study revealed eight factors which contribute to emotional and mental stability:

1. Absence of suspicion and resentment. Nursing a grudge is revealed as a major factor in unhappiness.

2. Living in the present. An unwholesome preoccupa-

tion with old mistakes and failures leads to depression.

3. Cooperating with life and taking advantage of whatever situation presents itself. Fighting conditions you cannot change wastes time and energy.

4. Staying involved with the living world. Becoming a recluse during periods of emotional stress extends the suffering.

5. Accepting the fact that everyone suffers from sorrow and misfortune. Indulging in self-pity when handed a raw deal expands the impact of the raw deal unnecessarily.

6. Cultivating love, honor, compassion, loyalty rather than selfishness.

7. Not expecting too much of self. Feelings of inadequacy are inevitable when the gap is wide between self-expectation and the ability to reach unrealistic goals.

8. Finding something bigger than yourself to believe in. Self-centered, egotistical people score lowest in any test to measure happiness.

PRAYER: Peace of mind, dear God, I know is available to me any time, any where, and under any circumstance. I may find it difficult to obtain sometimes during traumatic and high-stress times of my life. But I pray for it and ask You to sustain me during those times I cannot sustain myself. Amen.